HURLEY'S HEROES

Hurley's Heroes

UConn's Return to College Basketball's Elite

David Borges

Essex, Connecticut

An imprint of The Globe Pequot Publishing Group, Inc.
64 South Main St.
Essex, CT 06426
www.GlobePequot.com

Copyright © 2025 by David Borges

All rights reserved. No part of this book may be reproduced in any form or by any electronic or mechanical means, including information storage and retrieval systems, without written permission from the publisher, except by a reviewer who may quote passages in a review.

British Library Cataloguing in Publication Information available

Library of Congress Cataloging-in-Publication Data available

ISBN 9781493089673 (paperback) | ISBN 9781493089680 (epub)

Contents

Introduction ix

1   Leaks and Valleys 1
2   "I Build Programs" 7
3   Year 1: Ejections, Dejection 13
4   Year 2: It's Coming 19
5   Year 3: Back to the Big East 23

Very Superstitious 29

6   Bubble Ball 33
7   "Irregular Season" 39
8   Big Commitment 43
9   45:07 47
10 "Huge Win for the Program" 53
11 Buffaloed in Buffalo 57

Sad Story of Akok Akok 63

12 Portland Trail-blazing 67
13 January of Discontent 73
14 Back in Championship Form 79
15 "Go Win a Championship" 83
16 What Happens in Vegas 87
17 Avenging George Mason 91
18 "We've Got Our Own!" 95

Joey California 99

19 Art of Recruiting 101
20 One Big Loss 105
21 Repeat after Me 109
22 In the Phog 113
23 Saving Christmas 117
24 Back at No. 1 121
25 Rick Rolled 125
26 Another Jewel in the Crown 131
27 No Sleep 'til Brooklyn 135
28 A Boston Curb-Stomping 139
29 In the Mix for Six 143
30 Eclipsed! 147

Like Father, Like Son 153

31 "Me Season" 155
32 Say Goodbye to Hollywood 161
33 Wooden Dreams 167
34 Official Problems 171
35 Mayhem in Maui 175
36 Return to the Mainland 181

The New "Queen of Connecticut" 185

37 Season on the Brink 189
38 Next Man Up 193
39 Back-to-Back . . . Missed Free Throws? 197
40 "Best Coach in the Sport!" 201
41 Meet Mr. McNeeley 207
42 Jersey Barrier 211
43 "Karma" at MSG 217
44 A Chance at Salvation 221
45 Going Out with Honor 225

Contents

Groundhog Day 229
46 One Final Act 231
47 Comings and Goings 235
48 From Hunted Back to Hunter 239

Epilogue 245
Index 247

Introduction

"Don't write that, Dave!"

Dan Hurley would say this to me every now and then, sometimes after divulging some off-the-record information, sometimes after making an off-color remark at a public gathering.

He wasn't mean-spirited about it, but he always meant it. Hurley is extremely protective of any information about his team that he doesn't want to be made public. He doesn't let the local media into practices—shielding whatever plays he and his staff are drawing up, or however much he's yelling at his players—from prying eyes. He's very selective about what recruiting information he wants out there, once telling me that, while at Rhode Island, coaches would quickly jump into the fray for a recruit when they learned Hurley and his staff were on him.

He's remarkably superstitious and extremely intelligent, boasting both great street smarts (a product of gritty Jersey City, son of a probation officer) and book smarts (he taught history while also coaching hoops at St. Benedict's Prep!).

He carries an eternal chip on his shoulder, a product of growing up in the shadow of his father and older brother. Bob Hurley Sr. was the architect of the St. Anthony's High program in Jersey City, New Jersey, that won multiple state and national titles and churned out numerous future National Basketball Association (NBA) stars. He's one of the few high school coaches inducted into the Naismith Basketball Hall of Fame.

Bobby Hurley was one of his dad's biggest stars at St. Anthony's who wound up winning back-to-back national titles as a point guard at Duke, then playing in the NBA.

Dan Hurley also starred at St. Anthony's, then had a good, if rocky, five-year playing career at Seton Hall. That's where his playing career ended. It would take a lot as a coach for him to surpass the accomplishments of his father and older brother.

Dan is also incredibly entertaining, intentionally or not. He's seemingly incapable of holding a boring, run-of-the-mill press conference, either the day before a game (no matter how big) or in the minutes directly after one. One fellow writer once said it feels like Hurley is in a therapy session, or in confession, during his media confabs.

Would Hurley say, "Don't write that, Dave!" about this book? There may be a few items that he probably wishes would remain private. But overall, I don't think so.

Hurley became the 19th head coach in UConn men's basketball history on March 22, 2018. And I've been there every step of the way.

I've been there for all the good times: the Huskies' first trip to the National Collegiate Athletic Association (NCAA) tournament in six years, their big hits on the recruiting trail, the NBA Drafts where multiple Hurley recruits have been selected, the 2024 Big East tournament title, and, of course, the back-to-back national championship runs of 2023 and 2024. That entire 2023–2024 season, where UConn went 37–3, won the Big East regular-season and conference championships, then every NCAA tournament game by double digits, was a magical ride itself.

But I've been there for the bad times, too: the road trips to American Athletic Conference outposts like Greenville, North Carolina, and Tulsa, Oklahoma, where Hurley was once ejected during a mid-January game in front of a smattering of fans. The embarrassing home loss to St. Joseph's in Game 2 of Year 2, in front of barely 4,000 fans at Gampel Pavilion. The three losses in three days at the 2024 Maui Invitational (at least the weather was nice).

The state of the newspaper and media industry has vastly cut travel budgets for so many college basketball reporters. But I've been fortunate that Hearst Connecticut Media has bucked that trend. Other than the COVID-19 season of 2020–2021, I've been to all but a small handful of UConn games—home or road—from Madison Square Garden to Maui,

Introduction

Storrs to Seattle, Providence to Portland, Oregon. I missed both DePaul games in 2023–2024, the first shortly after my father had passed away, and the latter due to a snowstorm that canceled my flight to Chicago. I missed a game at Georgetown in 2022 due to contact tracing, after a fellow reporter tested positive for COVID. I may be forgetting one or two other missed games over the past seven years, but otherwise, like Johnny Cash once sang, "I've been everywhere, man."

Even in that COVID season, I covered the one road game where media was allowed, at Seton Hall, as well as the Big East tournament at Madison Square Garden (MSG) and the NCAA tournament in Indianapolis, chronicling the games far above courtside. I was even the lone UConn reporter to attend the 2021 NBA Draft, where James Bouknight was selected in the lottery. Turned out to be somewhat of a waste of time, as I wasn't even able to get Bouknight one-on-one and could have easily got his quotes like everyone else did, via a Zoom conference.

Still, the value of "being there" can't be understated. It gets you exclusive one-on-ones with Hurley, his assistants, and his players. It provides behind-the-scenes details of Hurley cussing out officials, or fans, from the sidelines or inside the bowels of a visiting arena. It provides colorful details of things that happen on the court, or even in the stands, that TV cameras don't pick up.

It doesn't always lead to smooth relations. I've had a few run-ins with Hurley, most notably after a Tweet I sent out following a game in January 2021 that was out of context and seemed to indicate there was dissension in the Huskies' ranks. That and more is chronicled in this book.

But overall, covering Dan Hurley since that March 22, 2018, afternoon has been a wild, entertaining, at times exhausting, but ultimately fulfilling ride.

Don't write this book, Dave? Sorry, this is my story of the Dan Hurley years at UConn, good times and bad.

1
Leaks and Valleys

Drip, drip, drip . . .

As rain poured down on Gampel Pavilion early in the day on November 13, 2019, the roof began leaking, a fitting analogy for a UConn men's basketball program that seemed to be coming apart at the seams.

The rain created puddles all over the basketball court, as well as doubt in Dan Hurley's mind whether the second game of his second season as UConn's head coach should be played later that evening.

"You could feel an ominous performance coming on," Hurley recalled.

And it wasn't just the dangerous court situation. The state of the team was in a bit of disarray. On the heels of the program's third straight losing season (but first under Hurley), the Huskies were without prized freshman recruit James Bouknight, who was sitting out the second of a three-game suspension after a bizarre, on-campus arrest a month earlier.

"You could tell the program was very fragile, in terms of the culture, the execution," Hurley remembered. "We were beginning a Year 2 back then with no real (transfer) portal. You couldn't remake your team the way people can now through NIL [name, image, and likeness] funding and/or the portal. So, you felt the fragile nature of the group as the ceiling was leaking."

Drip, drip, drip . . .

By the time Gampel's facilities operations team was called in, however, the rain had stopped. And so did the leaks.

Game on. Much to the chagrin of Hurley, a former 1,000-point scorer at Seton Hall who had never met a basketball game in which he didn't want to play or coach.

"Knowing what the team's mental state was going into that particular game, I wished the puddles would have kept forming, and maybe we just postpone, suspend the game, or just get a change of scenery," Hurley recalled. "It felt ominous to play the game there that night."

That was just the start.

The game against unheralded St. Joseph's certainly started ominously for UConn, which missed its first nine shots, allowing the Hawks to jump out to a 14–0 start. Behind some unconscious shooting by a 6-foot-5 guard named Ryan Daly, St. Joe's had built up a 27-point lead with 6½ minutes left to play—in the *first half*.

UConn gradually chipped away in the latter half and got to within three with just under 6 minutes to play. But St. Joe's finished it off for a 96–87 win. At the postgame press conference, Hurley was speechless for perhaps the first and only time of his UConn tenure.

"So, umm . . . ," he said, finally, after a long pause. "Year 2, Game 2 . . . we've obviously got a long way to go."

They sure did.

Year 1 had been no picnic, either. Hurley inherited a mess left by predecessor Kevin Ollie, the former UConn player and NBA veteran who had coached the Huskies to their fourth national championship just six years earlier.

UConn went 30–35 in Ollie's final two seasons at the helm before he was unceremoniously fired in March 2018, kicking off a long, ugly legal battle between him and the school that ultimately led to the university paying him more than $11 million for wrongful termination.

With much of the previous season's team still intact, UConn showed areas of promise in Hurley's first year at the helm. Still, the Huskies finished 16–17 overall, the first time the program had three straight losing seasons since before Hall of Famer and three-time national champion Jim Calhoun took over the program in 1986. Still stuck in the American

Athletic Conference (AAC), a league that no one wanted to be in after years in the electric, ultra-competitive Big East, Hurley's first year ended with a 39-point drubbing at the hands of Houston in the AAC tournament.

Now, it was the onset of Year 2, with puddles on the floor, panic in the locker room, and their best player banished to the bench.

Bouknight, a dynamic athlete and future NBA lottery pick, got his freshman year at UConn off to an inauspicious start, to say the least. In the early morning hours of September 27, 2019, Bouknight crashed a four-door sedan that belonged to a female UConn student into both a street sign and the back of a 2004 Toyota Sequoia.

Police detected an odor of alcohol emanating from Bouknight when he was pulled over. When he exited the car, Bouknight ran away from the officer. He was later charged with evading responsibility, interfering with a police officer, traveling too fast for conditions, and operating a motor vehicle without a license.

Ultimately, Bouknight was accepted into an accelerated rehabilitation program and ordered to make restitution to the owners of the property he damaged. His punishment from Hurley was arguably worse, subjected to the coach's fury during practices and being forced to sit out the Huskies' first three games of the season—including a big home game against Florida.

Certainly, Bouknight's absence didn't help the Huskies against St. Joe's. Still, there was no excuse for the loss.

Daly, a somewhat pudgy junior, was hitting 3-pointers from all over the place, just a few feet over the halfcourt line at times. He finished with a career-high 30 points and 5 treys.

"And," Hurley pointed out years later, "it wasn't like that St. Joe's team went on to a stellar season. They had a really tough year. That's what makes that even more painful, thinking about losing a game like that."

True, those 2019–2020 Hawks won just four more games the rest of the season and finished an unsightly 6–26 overall.

UConn, however, went the opposite way.

The Huskies, still without Bouknight, beat No. 15 Florida at home five days later. They would go on to their first winning season in three years, winning their last five and eight of their last 10 games. They flew down to Fort Worth, Texas, fully intent on winning the AAC tournament and getting the automatic NCAA tourney bid.

And they weren't planning on stopping there. Senior Christian Vital said prior to the season that his goal was to put up a fifth championship banner in the Gampel rafters. And in early March, despite how outlandish it might have sounded, he hadn't changed his tune.

"Until my eligibility is all used up," Vital said, "that's going to stay my goal."

Then, just a week later, the COVID-19 pandemic ended it all.

On the morning the Huskies were to begin play at Fort Worth's Dickies Arena (a far cry from the Big East tournament's home of Madison Square Garden), the AAC joined the rest of the leagues across the country in canceling their championship tournament.

Not long after, the NCAA tournament was canceled. Christian Vital's Joe Namath–like prediction of a fifth banner would have to wait, but not with him. He had a chance to return for a fifth season but chose to turn pro.

UConn's wait didn't last much longer.

In Year 2, Dan Hurley had returned some respectability to UConn men's basketball. The Huskies had notched impressive wins over Florida, Miami, Cincinnati, Memphis, and, in a bit of revenge from that 39-point trouncing a year earlier, a 77–71 win over Houston in their final home game of the season.

UConn finished 19–12 overall, their first winning season in four years, and 10–8 in the AAC. Oh, and about that AAC.

Over the prior summer, UConn was invited to rejoin the Big East, beginning in the 2020–2021 season. Well, not exactly "rejoin." The Huskies had never actually left the league. Syracuse, Louisville, Rutgers, West Virginia, and others had departed in prior years for football-oriented "Power 5" leagues like the Atlantic Coast Conference (ACC), Big 12, and Big 10. The "Catholic Seven" (basketball-centric Catholic schools Villanova, Seton Hall, Providence, Georgetown, St. John's,

Marquette, DePaul) banded together and bought the "Big East" name and use of Madison Square Garden for its conference tournament. UConn, Cincinnati, and South Florida renamed their league and joined forces with a collection of other schools from all over the map in a Conference of Misfit Toys.

Now, eight years later, UConn would again be in the Big East. Sure, it wasn't the same league as the Georgetown, Syracuse, St. John's powerhouses of the 1980s, or even the 1990s/2000s, when UConn was largely king.

But it was the Big East. Rekindled rivalries ignited with Villanova, which had taken over as the league's dominant team with national titles in 2016 and 2018, St. John's, and Georgetown.

It was bus rides to Providence or Seton Hall, rather than four-and-a-half-hour plane rides to Tulsa and Wichita. Sure, there were flights out to Omaha (Creighton) and Milwaukee (Marquette), but those programs were very good. Getting booed and verbally assaulted by 15,000 Creighton fans tops getting ejected from a game in front of a half-filled arena in Tulsa any day of the week.

And, of course, it was Madison Square Garden in Manhattan. Not Dickies Arena in Fort Worth.

Recruiting was picking up, even before the Big East news. Hurley had established a winning culture. Challenges remained ahead, but the program had gone from getting rained on through the Gampel roof and by Ryan Daley 3-pointers to promise and hope for success in the future.

And that success would come quicker than almost anyone could have imagined.

2
"I Build Programs"

When Dan Hurley was officially unveiled as UConn men's basketball's 19th head coach on March 22, 2018, he had a certified mess on his hands and a huge task ahead to get the program back to respectability. And further.

The program had suffered two losing seasons in a row for the first time since Jim Calhoun's first year on the job in 1986–1987. And they were often more than just losses. An unprecedented eight of the Huskies' 18 losses in 2017–2018 were by 20 points or more. The program that had won four national championships over the prior 20 seasons was uncompetitive at times.

It was just as ugly off the court. The team's academics were in disarray, in part a result of a coaching staff that wasn't keeping things in check. The Werth Family Champions Center, the team's practice facility, was just a few years old but wasn't nearly as state of the art as other top programs.

The roster was hardly brimming with talent, beaten down by two years of losing and physically underwhelming thanks to a lack of dedication in the weight room. One player, forward Kwintin Williams, had been recruited by Kevin Ollie and his staff based solely off watching him perform on YouTube videos.

"That," one person close to the program said at the time, "may be the best example of why Kevin deserved to be fired."

Hurley complained privately about what a mess he had inherited.

"He likes to complain," his dad, Bob Hurley Sr., said only half-jokingly. "His way of telling you things are going well is, 'We need a lot of work.'"

A lot of work *was* needed. But Dan Hurley had a blueprint. A blueprint to rebuild a program from the bottom up, one step at a time, one season at a time. It was a process that wouldn't happen overnight, but with which Hurley had already experienced success.

It went something like this:

- Year 1: Growing pains with players mostly recruited by the previous coach. Fan expectations needing to be tempered. And losses. Blowout losses. Last-second, heartbreaking losses. Road losses. A whole lot of road losses. But also some quality wins, and a glimpse of future potential.
- Year 2: More excruciating losses, mixed with a few nail-biting wins. The first influx of higher-level recruits, better athleticism, better defense, better culture. A better look, a better team.
- Year 3: The turning point, the biggest leap forward, with most of the roster filled with players Hurley recruited. Expectations to be at or near the top of the league.
- Year 4: NCAA tournament or bust, recruiting at a higher level.
- Year 5: NCAA tournament success, playing for conference championships, recruiting at a national level.
- Year 6: Seriously vying for a national championship.

Hurley was so adherent to the blueprint, so confident that it would work, that it almost felt like he would sacrifice a surprise season here or there just to stick to the plan.

"This is what it looks like," he'd often say, at any point of any season, his program almost always at about the place where Hurley expected it to be.

He had already had success turning around three different programs, the most recent over the prior six seasons about an hour down the road at Rhode Island.

"I Build Programs"

As at UConn, Hurley took over a reeling program when he was named head coach at the University of Rhode Island (URI) in 2012. The Rams had just gone 7–23 in their final season under Jim Baron. Just a couple of days after Hurley was hired, a talented freshman player was arrested for video voyeurism and was booted from the program.

Not long after that, the athletics department realized it had calculated the team's Academic Progress Rate (APR) number incorrectly, leading to more headaches for Hurley.

"A gift under the Christmas tree," he recalled, sarcastically.

The Rams went just 8–21 in Hurley's first season, though there were some positive signs: a double-overtime win over Auburn, 14 single-digit losses, and just one true blowout defeat.

In Year 2, Hurley brought in a strong recruiting class led by E. C. Matthews and Hassan Martin; the team went 14–18 and looked better. Year 3, Hurley brought in tough-as-nails Jared Terrell and Jarvis Garrett, and the Rams went 23–10 and to the National Invitational Tournament (NIT), where they lost to eventual champion Stanford in the second round.

This is what it was supposed to look like.

Of course, things don't always go precisely to plan. Blueprints sometimes must be revised. Year 4 at URI was supposed to end up in the Big Dance . . . until Matthews suffered a season-ending ACL injury in the first game of the season. The Rams finished 17–15 and out of the tournament.

But, after rebuking offers to coach Rutgers, the biggest school in his home state of New Jersey, Hurley stayed at URI and led the program to the NCAA tournament the next two seasons.

It was the first time in 19 years, when future NBA stars Cuttino Mobley, then Lamar Odom, were on the roster, that URI had back-to-back trips to the Big Dance.

And unlike those Rhody teams of 1997–1998 and 1998–1999, Hurley's 2016–2017 and 2017–2018 squads both advanced to the second round of the NCAA tourney. They beat future Big East rival Creighton in the first round in 2017 before falling to Oregon in a heartbreaker. In

2018, the Rams topped Oklahoma in the opening round before getting outclassed by a clearly superior Duke team.

No, the Rams never seriously contended for a national championship. That just doesn't happen at URI. But they won the Atlantic-10 tournament championship in 2017, then the regular season title in 2018.

Hurley's blueprint had worked.

Prior to URI, Hurley had worked his magic at Wagner, the small program on Staten Island that represented Hurley's first collegiate head coaching job. The season before Hurley's arrival in 2010, the Seahawks won a mere five games. By the time Hurley's whirlwind, two-year tenure at the school was over, Wagner had won 25 games in Hurley's final season, and he was on to URI.

Perhaps Hurley's most prolific program turnaround, his pièce de resistance to that point, hadn't come at the college level but, rather, at St. Benedict's Prep. Hurley took over the program, at a school located in a dilapidated section of Newark, New Jersey, in 2001 and built it up to where it was churning out future college and/or NBA stars like J. R. Smith, Tristan Thompson, Samardo Samuels, Lance Thomas, and Corey Stokes.

"It was like a college program," recalled George Blaney, the longtime UConn assistant coach who had been Hurley's head coach for two seasons when Hurley played at Seton Hall.

Hurley has called the process of rebuilding a program practically from scratch "addicting." Indeed, it almost seemed that he actually *preferred* the challenge of flipping a program back to relevance, rather than taking over a program at or near the top, like a Duke or a Kentucky (more on that later).

"The Carpenter," he would be dubbed by national college basketball journalist Jon Rothstein.

"I find the work to be incredibly fulfilling and rewarding," Hurley said. "All the mini-victories along the way: winning those recruiting battles, watching your players improve and change their habits, watching the crowds grow. People (at UConn) have experienced so much success, but there's something that's a lot of fun about the climb back up."

"I Build Programs"

After Hurley had finished his latest renovation at URI, he was one of the hottest coaching candidates in the country. Ultimately, his future came down to three choices: go rebuild programs at UConn or at Pittsburgh, or stay at URI, where he and his wife, Andrea, had made lifelong friends and were extremely happy.

The Monday after URI's season-ending loss to Duke, UConn athletic director David Benedict met with the Hurleys at their Saunderstown, Rhode Island, home with a contract offer. Later that day, the couple drove up to Providence to meet with Pittsburgh officials, who offered more money (well north of $3 million per year). The following day, URI came in with an offer.

Andrea had to get out of the house for a bit as Hurley wrestled with a decision that would change the family's lives. At one point they were going to stay at URI. Then, no, it's UConn. Then he called his agent, Jordan Bazant: "I'm not going to UConn anymore."

"Monday through Wednesday was a blur," Andrea recalled. "For something that should have been so exciting, it was awful. He second-guessed himself 27 times."

Finally, on presumably the 28th time, the decision was made. Hurley was moving on to yet another rebuilding challenge, and it wasn't in Pittsburgh.

"This is what I do," he told Andrea at the time. "I build programs."

The Dan Hurley era at UConn was about to begin.

3
Year 1
Ejections, Dejection

Jim Calhoun, the Naismith Hall of Famer and architect of perhaps the greatest program-build in college basketball history, was watching off to the side. The banners of Ray Allen, Emeka Okafor, Kemba Walker, and other past UConn greats stared down from the walls of the Werth Family Champions Center. But those weren't the most significant attendees at Dan Hurley's introductory press conference on March 23, 2018.

It was the presence of the entire roster of players from the previous 14–18, unmitigated disaster of a season that raised the most eyebrows that afternoon. Surely not all would remain following the firing of Kevin Ollie. Not in a day and age, even before the transfer portal, where players often fled a program at the first sign of change or challenge.

A year earlier, three players (Juwan Durham, Steve Enoch, and Vance Jackson) bolted Ollie's program after an ugly season that ended with a 16–17 record. A highly touted recruit, Makai Ashton-Langford, also backed out of his commitment to the Huskies and instead pledged to border rival Providence.

No way all of these players would stay and play for Hurley, who promised to be much more demanding than Ollie had over the prior few seasons, and perhaps even more than Calhoun in his heyday. And surely, Hurley wouldn't mind seeing a few of these players leave and filling their spots with recruits or transfers of his own choice.

Ultimately, they all stayed. Hurley did bring along with him Brendan Adams, who had committed to Hurley to play at URI but decommitted to join him in Storrs, along with a pair of transfers. But other than that, aside from a couple of departures via graduation, every player returned to play for Hurley.

"That was important to me," he said at the time. "I think it was real important for them to understand that I wasn't coming in looking to make transactions to change this place."

Most coaches may have done the opposite, but Hurley had a long-range plan. No need for bad optics that could ultimately hurt the already fragile psyche of the program—not to mention recruiting. Better to start bringing in his own, higher-quality recruits the following season.

Plus, the team wasn't likely to be very good, anyway. It was an odd mishmash of a roster composed of some talent sprinkled among several players probably not suited for high Division I play.

There were a couple of former top-rated recruits whose careers had been marred by injuries (Alterique Gilbert, Mamadou Diarra). There was a mercurial shooter in Christian Vital, who had clashed with Ollie numerous times (and would soon clash with Hurley quite a bit as well).

There was Kwintin Williams and his YouTube dunk highlight video.

And there was Jalen Adams, by far the most talented player on the roster. Adams had led the Huskies in scoring the prior season at 18.1 points per game and shown flashes of brilliance over his first three seasons at UConn: a career-high 34 points against Oklahoma State in Maui as a sophomore; a near triple-double against Tulsa as a junior; and, of course, a miraculous, 75-foot shot as a freshman to send UConn's opening-round, AAC tournament game against Cincinnati into overtime. The Huskies would ultimately win the game in four overtimes, then the tournament to secure an NCAA tourney bid.

It would be their last for a while.

But for all his talent, Adams had a carefree attitude that seemingly didn't jibe with Hurley's fiery approach, and that was evident a few times in Year 1.

It all got off to a nice start. After UConn won its first two games at Gampel as part of the 2K Classic, the event shifted to Madison Square Garden, where the Huskies faced old Big East rival Syracuse.

Few programs annoy UConn fans more than the Orange. Maybe Duke, but that's about it. And so, when Adams and Gilbert each scored 16 points, and Tarin Smith and Eric Cobb combined for 27 off the bench to lead the Huskies to an 83–76 win over Jim Boeheim & Co., the Hurley era was off and running.

At the end of the game, in a hilarious scene, Hurley celebrated wildly, chest-bumping Adams on the sidelines before realizing Boeheim was approaching and immediately composing himself to shake the Hall of Fame coach's hand. It was an early glimpse of Hurley's unbridled passion on the sidelines, as well as the future capacity of the program for big wins (Syracuse was ranked No. 15 at the time) at the World's Most Famous Arena.

And it all came to an immediate, crashing halt the following night at MSG, when the Huskies were trounced 91–72 by Iowa, led by National Player of the Year candidate Luka Garza. Hurley wasn't around for the end of this one, ejected from the game after picking up his second technical foul with less than 2 minutes to play.

It was Hurley's first ejection as UConn coach, in just his fourth game. It would hardly be his last. Indeed, Hurley breathed fire on the sidelines, not unlike Jim Calhoun, bristling with intensity and pent-up emotions.

This is a man, after all, who had been ejected from his own closed-door scrimmage early in his career at Rhode Island.

Ultimately, that win over Syracuse in the third game of the season was probably the highlight of Year 1 under Hurley. The Huskies would fall to Arizona in Hartford; get bullied by Florida State in Newark, New Jersey; and get smoked by Villanova (a non-league opponent at the time) at MSG.

In UConn's AAC season-opener on January 2, 2019, in Tampa against South Florida, the Huskies got off to a strong start, leading by 13 points late in the first half and 33–25 at halftime. Adams was hot and happy, strumming an imaginary air guitar each time he knocked down a 3 (a common celebration by college players at the time).

Then came the second half. Perhaps a bit overconfident, the Huskies watched their lead slip away with sloppy play and a lack of leadership. A promising start to Hurley's AAC tenure ended in a 76–68 loss to a perennially subpar team.

Hurley was furious. The following morning, he called a former college coach to rant about the team's lack of killer instinct, particularly Adams and his Eddie Van Halen air-guitar impressions. Three days later, in Hartford, the Huskies fell to University of Central Florida (UCF) 65–53, despite outrebounding 7-foot-6 monster Tacko Fall and the Knights by 14, including an incredible 17–0 on the offensive boards.

"I don't think I've ever seen that before," UCF coach Johnny Dawkins mused afterward.

Maybe not, but the Huskies were 0–2 in league play, and Hurley's frustrations were growing. They came to a head a couple of weeks later in Tulsa—on Hurley's 46th birthday, no less.

About midway through the second half, both Hurley and Tulsa coach Frank Haith were hit with technical fouls. Hurley seemed to go over and try to shake hands with Haith. More words were exchanged and, at some point, both coaches got hit with a second "T" and were ejected from the game.

"We were looking to come together, shake hands, and show some sportsmanship there," Hurley insisted. "But then, the mishandling of it led to an embarrassment."

Haith seemed to agree.

"It was competitive banter," the Tulsa coach said. "Both coaches are competitors and both coaches were trying to help their team. I think it started out like that. I don't think it escalated to both of us being ejected, and that's disappointing."

Ironically, Hurley and Haith had a good relationship; their wives even socialized at times in the off-season. More important, Tulsa wound up winning the game 89–83, improving to 5–0 against the Huskies since the beginning of the AAC six years earlier.

Happy birthday, Dan!

On a cold, snowy night in Tulsa, in front of fewer than 4,000 fans at something called the Reynolds Center, their coach ejected for the second time of the season, and a fifth straight loss to a program that had made the NCAA tournament just twice over the prior 16 years, it was about as far away as possible from winning national championship blowouts in front of 80,000 fans in Houston or Phoenix.

And yet, here the Huskies were.

The rest of the season plodded on. Hurley had friction with some players. Sid Wilson was suspended early in the season. The always emotional Vital was more than Hurley could handle at times. After one road loss, Hurley could be heard cursing out Vital to UConn sports information director Phil Chardis, insisting that Vital not be allowed to talk to the media.

As Hurley's blueprint had lined out, there were blowout losses (Iowa, Villanova, at Temple, at Southern Methodist University [SMU]) and excruciating losses (by two points at Cincinnati; by four at home to Cincinnati, thanks largely to a 30-foot prayer with 12 seconds left by Connecticut native Cane Broome, of all people; a two-point loss at Wichita State). And road losses. Lots of road losses. The Huskies finished 1–8 away from home.

In the AAC tournament in Memphis, UConn got a bit of revenge on South Florida with an 80–73 win behind 25 points from Vital and 19 from Adams. The following day, however, UConn was annihilated by top-seeded Houston by nearly 40 points. The Cougars, coached by Kelvin Sampson, were the type of team Hurley aspired his Huskies to be someday: tough, athletic, defensive minded, with a strong culture. It was painfully evident that day on March 15, 2019, in Memphis, that the Huskies were a long way from all of that.

4

Year 2

It's Coming

Dan Hurley sat at the podium on Saturday, January 18, 2020, in Philadelphia, a familiar look of disappointment on his face, tinged with a hint of optimism and confidence in his voice.

His Huskies had just lost to Villanova. Again. A reminder that Villanova was still king of the Big East Conference, the league UConn had once dominated and, in a year, hoped to start dominating once again.

But 'Nova was still king, winning the third and final installment of a three-game series over three seasons with the Huskies that began in January 2018 in Hartford, continued in December 2018 at Madison Square Garden, and now concluded on this night at Philly's Wells Fargo Center.

The first two matchups weren't pretty for UConn: an 81–61 trouncing with Kevin Ollie still at the helm, yet another 20-point loss for the Huskies in a season full of them. By the end of the season, UConn was 14–18, Ollie was fired, and Villanova had won its second national championship in three years.

In Year 1 of Hurley, it was an 81–58 demolition at the hands of the defending national champs at MSG, a place that typically brought great memories for UConn fans.

But this third game was different. Before 16,723 fans inside the home of the Philadelphia 76ers and Flyers, unranked UConn gave the

14th-ranked Wildcats all they could handle—and a glimpse of what the future could look like.

Neither team led by more than seven points throughout the game. Ultimately, UConn led for 18 minutes and 22 seconds of play; Villanova led for 18 minutes and 52 seconds.

But when it mattered most, Villanova had the 61–55 lead—and the win. Again.

Excruciating.

The Huskies were getting closer, and Hurley felt it. And after the latest, closest loss to Villanova that Saturday night in Philly, Hurley put it into words.

Wrapping up an 8½-minute postgame press conference, Hurley provided a mic-drop moment for the ages.

"People better get us now, that's all," he warned. "They better get us now. Because it's coming."

Bold. Confident. The latest iconic quote from a UConn coach, right there with Ollie's "We're gonna take the stairs" or any number of Jim Calhoun barbs over his 26-year career.

It's coming. When would it come? Hurley wouldn't elaborate.

Villanova's time had certainly come and wasn't about to end too soon. No program had taken advantage of the void UConn left once the Big East folded in 2013 more than Villanova. In its first 34 seasons in the Big East, 'Nova had won the league's regular-season championship just four times. There was a miraculous, 1985 national championship victory over Georgetown tucked in there, but by and large, while 'Nova was certainly in the upper echelon of the Big East, it was rarely at the top.

That space was largely reserved for UConn throughout the 1990s and 2000s. Beginning with their "Dream Season" under Jim Calhoun in 1990, the Huskies won the Big East tournament seven times before the league's breakup. Villanova won just once (beating UConn, ironically, in 1995).

Even after UConn was relegated to the American Athletic Conference in 2013–2014 and Villanova remained in the Big East, the Huskies still owned the upper hand. In their march to a fourth national title in 2014, the Huskies dusted off 'Nova along the way, 77–65 in a Round-of-32 bout up in Buffalo, New York.

Still, with UConn out of the league, the Wildcats won four of five Big East tournaments between 2015 and 2019 while the Huskies largely languished in the AAC. There were also two more national titles for Villanova, in 2016 and 2018, as it became the nation's model program and Jay Wright the model coach (literally and figuratively).

Now, more competitive or not, a third straight loss to Wright & Co. And it was the latest in a long line of losses to high-caliber teams since Hurley had taken over the reins.

It's coming? It didn't come immediately.

UConn lost its next two games, at Houston and at home against Tulsa. In fact, the Huskies lost five of their next nine games. Then came a five-game, regular season–ending winning streak. Included among those wins was that 77–71 win at Gampel over No. 21 Houston, Hurley's first win in four tries against Kelvin Sampson's program.

Following that victory on Senior Day, Christian Vital addressed the Gampel crowd briefly, noting, "It's been a crazy four years for me, personally . . . I've got to thank that man Dan Hurley, man. We had some brutal times together. But he came in here on a mission . . . we've had a lot of ups and downs these past two years, but what we've done this year is special. But we're not done yet!" he quickly added.

Then, Vital, the most prolific 3-point sniper in AAC history, shouted, "Sniper, out!," dropped the mic, and walked off the floor to thunderous applause.

Unfortunately for Vital, it was the final time he'd walk off the Gampel floor. The NCAA dropped the rest of the season a week later.

After a narrow win over Tulane inside a glorified high school gym in New Orleans to close out its regular season, UConn went to the AAC tournament hot, and with clear thoughts of an NCAA tourney bid dancing in their heads. But on March 12, the day the tourney was supposed to start, COVID-19 reared its ugly head.

One league after another, started a couple of days earlier by the Ivy League, began cancelling their respective championship tournaments, and the AAC joined the fray. The Big East was among the last to cancel its tournament, at halftime of its opening game.

Soon after, the NCAA tournament was canceled as well. Just like that, it was all over.

Sniper, out.

Vital finished his career as UConn's 10th all-time leading scorer, as well as the all-time top 3-point leader in AAC history.

He also had the ignominious distinction of being the first four-year Husky player not to reach a postseason tournament (not even the National Invitation Tournament [NIT]) in more than 40 years, since Gerry Besselink, a center who played in Storrs from the 1983–1984 season to Calhoun's first season at the helm in 1986–1987.

But Hurley was still grateful for the contributions Vital made as both he and the program matured. He was grateful for guys like Isaiah Whaley, who Hurley benched for much of his first season at the helm, but who ultimately emerged as "The Wrench," a do-it-all player who played as hard as anyone. Guys like Tyler Polley, who overcame a torn ACL to become a quiet leader and occasional dead-eye shooter, and Josh Carlton, who Hurley turned into the AAC's Most Improved Player after first getting a chance with him as a sophomore.

These were the guys who helped the Huskies get over the hump, even if they had no championship rings to show for it.

It's coming? Thanks to these guys, it most certainly was.

And so was a return to the Big East.

5

Year 3

Back to the Big East

For all his cockiness and swagger, Dan Hurley is often somewhat self-deprecating about his own playing career at Seton Hall.

Yet every now and then over his first season at UConn's helm, he'd point out that he was a 1,000-point scorer in the Big East.

"The *real* Big East," he'd add, for emphasis.

Indeed, while Hurley was a scrappy point guard for the Pirates from 1991 to 1996, the Big East was home to dangerous denizens and future Hall of Famers like Allen Iverson, Alonzo Mourning, and, of course, UConn's own Ray Allen, not to mention stars like Kerry Kittles, John Wallace, and UConn's Donyell Marshall.

The current Big East clearly didn't quite live up to Hurley's standards after he took over at UConn, even if the league still routinely got five or six NCAA tourney bids each year and had spawned national-champion Villanova teams in 2016 and 2018.

And so, when news got out over the summer of 2019 that UConn was being invited back to the Big East, Hurley had to change his tune a bit. On June 27, a Madison Square Garden press conference featuring Hurley and UConn women's basketball Hall of Fame coach Geno Auriemma, Big East commissioner Val Ackerman and others formally welcomed UConn back to the league—even if it wouldn't be official for another year.

"So, is this the '*real* Big East?,'" reporters asked Hurley that day.

The coach smiled, chuckled, and insisted he only used that phrase in the past when recruiting against Big East programs while at URI and UConn.

"It really is like a dream come true," Hurley told the media. "It's almost like getting hired again."

Indeed, Dan Hurley *is* the Big East. Born in Jersey City, New Jersey, in the shadow of the league's 1980s heyday of Patrick Ewing, Chris Mullin, Pearl Washington, John Thompson, Louie Carnesecca, and Jim Boeheim.

While playing at Seton Hall, he remembered getting chills just seeing the famous white towel draped around Thompson's shoulders when the Pirates played Georgetown. While teaching and coaching at St. Benedict's Prep in the 2000s, he used to find a substitute for his afternoon class so he could sneak out and catch some Big East tournament action.

"The Big East is where UConn belongs," Hurley said that June day. "The league is a great fit for us. The history we have together, UConn has been such a huge part of the history of the conference. It's just a perfect fit."

Of course, this wasn't the Big East of Hurley's youth. Or even of a decade earlier. No more Syracuse. No more Louisville. No more Pittsburgh or Boston College or Notre Dame or West Virginia.

But it was a big step up from the American in competition, and for its fan base. UConn fans held a somewhat irrational hatred of the AAC, where the best rivalry was probably Cincinnati—never a truly sexy opponent when it shared the Big East with UConn. Programs like SMU, Tulsa, East Carolina, even Houston, simply didn't spark the same excitement as Villanova, Georgetown, St. John's, or Providence.

"Replace a Tulsa trip with a Providence trip, right there it feels better," Hurley said that day.

The move was going to benefit UConn in so many ways. A few months after that "welcome back" press conference, the league's coaches converged at the Garden for Big East Media Day. UConn, of course, was still a year away from joining the Big East. But the league's coaches, for the most part, weren't exactly looking forward to that.

"I can't tell recruits, 'You know what it's like to play at Tulane and East Carolina and those places?'" 10th-year Seton Hall coach Kevin Willard said, seemingly half-jokingly. "It doesn't work anymore."

Willard tended to be a bit playful and sarcastic with the press, so it was hard to tell how serious he was when he continued: "No one asked me, but I would not have given them the vote. I would have told them to stay away. Just because I know what type of job Danny's going to do. I know what a great program it is. We're now going to a 20-game schedule in this league, so it's going to make the conference better and harder. But I think overall, everyone's excited to bring them back."

Providence's Ed Cooley was far more blunt.

"I think it's going be a bear to deal with," said Cooley, who was entering his ninth year as head coach of his hometown school. "They have a very good staff there, and Danny is one of the better coaches in the country. Regionally, with Providence College and Seton Hall, in particular—with a little bit of St. John's—we're gonna have our hands full when it comes to competing against them."

In fact, Cooley seemed to think the Big East did UConn a favor by taking it back in.

"I think we gave Connecticut new life," he said. "We gave their fan base new life. They finally came to the conclusion that they are a basketball-centric school. They poured all their money in football, and in my opinion, it was going into a hole."

"When you've become a national brand in one sport and try to parlay into something it isn't," Cooley added, "shame on you for making the decision upfront."

Yikes.

Patrick Ewing, the legendary former Georgetown center who was entering his third year as the Hoyas' head coach, was more diplomatic.

"It is what it is," he said, from the Garden floor where he had furbished a Hall of Fame career as the New York Knicks' center. "They're here, they're here to stay, and it's our job as coaches to recruit and try to get the best players we can for our programs. And the players, it's their job to compete and play against whoever's there."

Jay Wright, with a pair of recent national titles in his hip pocket, seemed least worried.

"I think everything's positive, I really do," he said. "I think it enhances the brand. In recruiting, Connecticut will get involved with all the guys we're all involved with, and we'll all compete against each other. It's just going to increase the pool. There will be kids growing up in Connecticut, following the Big East, and they might wind up playing at Georgetown. That's what happened in the old Big East, and I think the same thing's going to happen."

There was no question that UConn's recruiting would significantly improve now that it was returning to the Big East. Top players from New York, Philadelphia, New Jersey, and the "DMV" (DC, Maryland, Virginia) were far more inclined to play in an East Coast–centric league rather than taking flights to outposts like Greenville, North Carolina; Tulsa; and Wichita. And, of course, it was a better league than the AAC, with tons more cachet.

Hurley acknowledged that, yet bristled at the suggestion that the Big East alone was going to cure any of the program's perceived recruiting woes. Hurley had already brought in a national top-20 recruiting class, led by future NBA lottery pick James Bouknight, long before any Big East rumors had popped up. He was extremely proud of his and his staff's ability to recruit, to the point where, starting at URI and continuing at UConn, he was very tight-lipped about his recruiting targets, certain that other programs would jump on any recruit when they found out Hurley was after him.

But even UConn's Class of 2020 commits, like Albany, New York's Andre Jackson Jr., admitted that the move to the Big East greatly aided his decision to commit to Storrs. The Huskies would soon add Adama Sanogo, a 6-foot-9 forward from Mali who played at the Patrick School in New Jersey and appeared ticketed to Seton Hall before Hurley and the Huskies swooped in (seemingly justifying Kevin Willard's fears).

The machine was revving up. The blueprint was on schedule, aided by an unexpected bump up in league affiliation.

It was coming. Of course, the Huskies still had to get through that last hurrah in the AAC in 2019–2020. Hurley didn't talk much about the Big East throughout that season, even featuring a cardboard cutout of the AAC tournament trophy at every UConn practice as an enticement for the Huskies' goal at hand.

And UConn certainly seemed like it could wave goodbye to the AAC with a bang after that regular season–ending five-game winning streak, heading into the league tournament hot and utterly confident that it would win.

The pandemic ended all that. Now, it was time to focus on the return to the Big East in the season ahead.

When (if?) that season would even begin.

Very Superstitious

One of the quirks of Dan Hurley—and there are many—is a rabid superstitiousness that is, if nothing else . . . complicated.

"It's my armor," Hurley has said.

He's always been that way. While at the University of Rhode Island, Hurley would burn sage on the floor of the Ryan Center before the start of each season to ward off evil spirits. He also put garlic in the left corner of the gym after the Rams kept getting beaten by buzzer-beaters from the left corner. And it was successful. He has continued to burn sage and place garlic under the stands around Gampel Pavilion and XL Center at the start of each season.

But that's hardly where his superstitions end.

At URI, he wouldn't eat the day before a game and, sometimes, wouldn't eat the day after if the team lost. Hurley said he'd lose 10, sometimes 15 pounds over the course of a season.

He has a ritual that he must hit two halfcourt shots in a row before the start of each practice. UConn players have to wait outside in the hallway until Hurley makes two in a row.

At his home in Glastonbury, Connecticut, Hurley has a "weirdo room" that houses all his various "chotchkes"—a spiritual statue of Archangel Michael, the Holy Bible, Marvel and DC Comic superhero paraphernalia, and inspirational quotes and posters of Michael Jordan, Kobe Bryant, and others on the wall for further motivation.

In the corner of that room, he revealed during a 60 Minutes *feature in 2025, is a stuffed-animal zebra facing the wall, symbolizing his often-contentious relationship with referees.*

Hurley spends a lot of time meditating in the room, which is off-limits to anyone but close family and team members.

Then there's the underwear.

On UConn's 2023 national championship run, Hurley's undergarments became national news. His wife, Andrea, told the New York Post that Hurley wore the same outfit for each of the Huskies' six victories: navy suit jacket, blue checkered shirt, navy socks . . . and a pair of red boxer shorts, emblazoned with cartoon dragons.

In 2024, Hurley sported a pair of wolf-themed undies through the Huskies' Big East tournament title. But he decided to "retire" those until the following season and go back to the dragons for the NCAA tournament.

And worry not, Hurley's underwear was clean for each game. Andrea toted a portable washing machine, bought for her by the Hurleys' eldest son, Daniel, on each of UConn's road trips, and washed the undies in her hotel room, drying them off with a hairdryer.

During the 2024 NCAA tournament, Hurley also revealed to CT Insider *that he eats M&M candies prior to each game. Eight M&M's, seven if he drops one on the floor. And only specific colors, ones that don't include the color of that night's opposing team's uniform.*

No orange before Syracuse. No blue before Villanova or Georgetown. No red before St. John's.

It is also imperative for Hurley to have mushroom coffee on the sidelines. Directly after opening tip-off in a March 10, 2024, game at Providence, Cam Spencer knocked Hurley's cup of coffee over while chasing down a loose ball.

Hurley was thrown completely off-kilter, not even calling offensive or defensive plays the next two possessions until his cup was refilled with mushroom coffee. It was. UConn won.

On January 5, 2025, at Gampel (again against Providence), Hurley and Friar coach Kim English joined other Big East coaches in sporting a sweater on the sidelines in honor of Lou Carnesecca, the longtime St. John's coach who had died a month earlier at age 99. Carnesecca was known for his somewhat garish sweaters while leading St. John's for 24 seasons.

Hurley sported a white sweater with a blue and red design on the front, in lieu of his typical blazer. UConn missed nine of its final 10 shots of the first half and trailed by 12 at the break, by far its biggest halftime deficit of the season. Something had to change.

Hurley couldn't change the sweater at halftime out of respect for Carnesecca, but he did switch socks. He also went from thick-rimmed glasses to thinner-rimmed frames for the latter half.

UConn rallied back to win 87–84.

6
Bubble Ball

The COVID-19 pandemic played havoc with the entire world through the spring, summer, and fall of 2020, and the sports world was hardly immune.

The NBA, whose regular season's start was delayed, held its finals inside a "bubble" at Disney World in Orlando, where teams stayed in hotels and played at arenas inside the resort. All games were closed to the public.

Major League Baseball's season also started late and was condensed from the usual 162 games to 60, also with no fans allowed at games. For the first time ever, the World Series was held at a neutral site, Globe Life Field in Arlington, Texas, where a limited amount of fans were allowed to attend.

Even the mighty National Football League (NFL) held many of its regular season games inside empty stadiums.

That fall, the UConn football team became the only Division I, Football Bowl Subdivision program in the nation to cancel its entire season. That was not going to be the case with the UConn basketball teams. Still, the start of what would be a strange season ("bizarre," as Hurley frequently liked to say) got off to a late start.

UConn didn't open its season until November 25, nearly a month later than usual, with a 102–75 romp over nearby Central Connecticut State. The game was held at Gampel Pavilion, as all of the Huskies' home games would be that season. And, like every Husky home game, there were no paying fans in attendance, only small groups of family of players and staff.

It was bizarre. Instead of the typical home and away team benches along one sideline, three rows of about 15 chairs each were set up on the opposite sideline, allowing for social distancing for players not in the game. The players didn't have to wear masks, but the coaches did, raising Hurley's ire.

Of course, Hurley stretched the definition of "wearing a mask." At times, his mask was pulled down as if it was a chinstrap, allowing him to better yell out commands to his players, or at the referees.

It was all kind of ironic, because Hurley is somewhat of a germophobe. He diligently wore a mask in public places like supermarkets or restaurants during COVID, sometimes even rubber gloves as well.

Media was allowed to attend games but sat up in Section 8 of Gampel, way up in the southwest corner of the building, among the worst seats in the house. Postgame press conferences were held on Zoom calls, meaning the media didn't actually have to attend games. And sometimes individual members didn't, instead watching the games on TV and jumping on the postgame Zoom call afterward.

In fact, every interaction between media and Hurley and/or players that season was done through Zoom. That included media availabilities held the day before games. For home games, these had typically been held at Gampel (or sometimes XL Center in Hartford, if that's where UConn was playing the following night). For road games, the traveling media (usually no more than three or four members, sometimes just one or two) would usually interview Hurley and a player or two at the team's hotel, shortly after they had arrived the night before a game.

Now, it was Zoom, Zoom, Zoom all the way. Personal interaction between the media and the team was almost nonexistent, which led to occasional hostility along the way.

UConn won its first two games of the season, then bussed about a half-hour down the road for the three-game Legends Classic at Mohegan Sun Arena—or "Bubbleville," as the tournament was being called. The teams would all stay at the Mohegan Sun's hotel, but every player would have to test negative for COVID each day to play.

The Huskies were slated to face Vanderbilt and Scottie Pippen Jr., son of the NBA Hall of Famer, in their opener. But Vandy withdrew from the event on the eve it was supposed to begin due to positive COVID tests.

On December 3, UConn topped USC 61–58 inside the empty arena. A date with NC State was slated two days later. This time, it was UConn's turn to cancel due to COVID, after a member of the program tested positive. Per university protocol, all team activities were put on hold until contact tracing and additional testing was completed.

The Huskies' next three games (against St. John's and at Georgetown and Providence) were all postponed. Such was college basketball in 2020–2021.

UConn finally returned to the floor on December 20 at Gampel in what would be its first Big East game since a stirring, overtime win over Providence on March 9, 2013. No fans were in the building, but another classic unfolded, this time against ninth-ranked Creighton. And once again it went into overtime, as R. J. Cole missed a pair of free throws with 11 seconds left in regulation and Creighton's Damien Jefferson hit a tough jumper as the clock expired.

The Bluejays ultimately prevailed 76–74 despite a Herculean effort from James Bouknight. The sophomore guard poured in 40 points, the most by a UConn player since 7-foot Amida Brimah dunked 40 on lowly Coppin State in 2014, and the most by a Husky in Big East play since Donyell Marshall dropped 42 (twice!) on St. John's in 1994.

It was also the second-highest scoring effort in any player's Big East debut, surpassed only by the 41 scored by Marquette's Steve Nowak on January 3, 2006—ironically, against UConn.

More to the point, it firmly introduced James Bouknight to the world. Seven months later, Bouknight was selected by Charlotte with the No. 11 overall pick in the 2021 NBA Draft.

"James became a lottery pick when he dropped 40 in his first Big East game," Hurley said the day before the draft.

Perhaps, but the remainder of the season wound up being a somewhat rocky one for Bouknight. He injured his elbow during a game at Marquette on January 5, 2021. The Huskies still won thanks to 23 points off the bench from Tyler Polley, but Bouknight missed the next couple of games and, on January 13, underwent elbow surgery.

He wouldn't play again for more than a month.

Still, the Huskies got by, winning four straight (in between two more postponements) and earning their first Top 25 ranking in four years heading into a January 18 bout with St. John's at Gampel.

UConn jumped out to a 21–7 start, led by eight inside the final 12 minutes, and never trailed at all until the final 4 minutes, 16 seconds—during which it never led. St. John's rallied for a 74–70 win to improve to a mere 3–6 in league play.

Hurley made an odd decision in that one. Adama Sanogo, the freshman center, was having his best game as a collegian, scoring 12 points in 17 minutes of action. With 12:46 remaining and UConn up by eight, Sanogo was lifted from the game during a time-out.

He never returned. And the Red Storm stormed back to hand the Huskies what Hurley termed a "brutal, brutal loss."

Did it have to be that way? Sanogo wasn't injured or in foul trouble. He could have returned to the game at any time and continued dominating inside.

But St. John's had switched to a small lineup, and Hurley felt there was no one for the 6-foot-9 Sanogo to guard. The coach may have been overthinking this one a bit.

On the postgame Zoom call, Sanogo was asked about the situation.

"At the end of the game, I think I should have played a little bit more," the soft-spoken Mali native said. "But they were playing four guards, so it was a little bit tough for me to be in at the end of the game."

And here's where Zoom calls, as opposed to in-person press conferences, could cause problems.

One reporter, in a rush to post Sanogo's comments as quickly as possible on Twitter, only posted the first part: "At the end of the game, I think I should have played a little bit more."

And as can happen on social media, it caused an immediate firestorm. UConn fans felt Sanogo's comments clearly showed he was upset at not playing. Upset at Hurley. Dissension in the ranks, no doubt.

Of course, it wasn't true. About 15 minutes later, after transcribing Sanogo's entire Zoom interview, the reporter posted Sanogo's full quote, adding the latter part about four guards and how it would have been tough for him to be in the game.

That reporter, by the way, was me.

The damage had been done. When Hurley found out about the initial Twitter post and the firestorm it created, he was very upset. And he had a right to be.

No doubt, my initial post was misleading. There was no ill intent, no attempt to create a controversy, just an attempt to post a quote as quickly as possible, in real time. But I should have waited until after transcribing Sanogo's interview and posted his entire quote for proper context.

I was wrong. But then, so was the reaction of Hurley and UConn.

Five days later, after a loss at Creighton during which Hurley had received a technical foul, I asked on the postgame Zoom call to explain the reason for the "T."

"None of your business, Dave!" Hurley screamed. *"None of your business!!!"*

Hurley might have been upset by the loss, or even the question, but this was odd. He was typically open and upfront with any question he was asked and had yet to really explode at a media member over his first two and a half seasons the way Jim Calhoun frequently had over his 26-year career.

I soon found out that he was still fuming at the Sanogo Twitter post. Hurley prided himself on running a program with an extremely close, family-like culture. Anything that made it appear otherwise, particularly via the vast reach of social media, would upset him. And perhaps more important, anything that might hurt recruiting would *really* upset him.

The next morning, I sent him a voicemail as well as a text, apologizing for the Tweet while explaining why it happened. The last thing I wanted to do was make a player look bad. Hurley never responded, though I later learned he was appreciative that I had reached out. I also apologized on Twitter.

Then, I found out that UConn had decided to ignore me on Zoom calls, or at least make me wait until the end of each call. This was a bit immature, unprofessional, and petty.

Was this really going to continue throughout the rest of the season, making it much harder to do my job on a very competitive beat?

This 2020–2021 season, in so many ways, was not very fun. For anyone.

7

"Irregular Season"

My freeze-out by Hurley and his staff only lasted about a week before my Zoom questions were answered in proper order and things got back to normal. Well, as normal as possible in this strange season.

Amid more game postponements and a couple of losses, UConn was no longer even receiving Associated Press Top 25 votes by February 16. Then, it received some good news: James Bouknight, out for the past six weeks with an injured elbow, returned and immediately announced his presence with authority in a home game against Providence.

Bouncing off the bench for the first and only time of the season, Bouknight quickly displayed the speed and athleticism the Huskies had sorely missed over their prior eight games. Just a few minutes after entering the game, Bouknight threw down a one-handed, putback dunk that would have sent Gampel in a tizzy had fans been allowed at the game.

(It was probably only the second-best dunk of Bouknight's career, however. Nothing could top his one-handed alley-oop dunk off an off-the-mark lob from Jalen Gaffney the prior season at East Carolina University [ECU] on February 29, 2020. Leap year, appropriately enough).

Bouknight's return sparked a Husky victory, and after (yet another) loss at Villanova, UConn won its next four games. As they had the prior season, the Huskies entered their conference tournament playing their best ball of the season. And this time the conference tournament would be played at Madison Square Garden, not Dickies Arena, even if only a smattering of fans were allowed in the building (the same might have been true at Dickies, pandemic or no pandemic, a year earlier!).

The Huskies dusted off lowly DePaul in their opening game by 34 points. Only problem? Just under 2 minutes into the second half, Bouknight left the game with leg cramps. After being tended to by trainer James Doran, he returned to the game a few minutes later.

Then, just as quickly, UConn's leading scorer was lying prone on the sideline in obvious pain, suffering from full-body cramps. Ultimately, he was helped to his feet and carried back to the locker room by Doran and strength coach Mike Rehfeldt. He never returned to the game.

Hurley downplayed it a bit, saying Bouknight simply had to hydrate better before, during, and after games. He was ready to go the next night against Creighton in the tournament semifinals, which looked more like the de facto championship game between two red-hot teams.

The game lived up to its billing: a back-and-forth, Friday night battle that featured eight ties and a pair of lead changes in the second half. But for the first time in nearly three weeks, UConn didn't own the final lead.

With 5:07 left in regulation, UConn led 53–48 and appeared in good shape to head to the Big East tourney championship game for the first time since 2011. But with about 4½ minutes left, senior point guard R. J. Cole, the heart and soul of the team, went crashing to the floor, banging his head, and left the court bloodied and not to return.

Perhaps frazzled by the loss of their leader, the Huskies looked rudderless, missing their final seven field goal attempts. Creighton outscored UConn 11–3 over that final 5:07 to notch the victory.

Afterward, Isaiah Whaley, "the Wrench," was in tears. Bouknight was disconsolate after what he later termed his "worst game in a UConn uniform."

He finished with 14 points on 4-for-14 shooting and turned the ball over four times.

"Our guys are crushed," Hurley said on the Zoom call afterward.

Hurley was, too. Obviously, his ultimate goal was to win national championships. But as his blueprint started to take shape, Big East regular-season and tournament championships seemed far more tangible

"Irregular Season"

in the short term. He *was* the Big East, after all, and winning a league title was everything to him.

The Huskies fell short on both counts, finishing third in the regular season at 11–6, then getting popped by Creighton for the third time this season.

Making it even more painful was that UConn would have met up with upstart Georgetown in the finals on Saturday night. The Huskies had handled Patrick Ewing's Hoyas twice during the regular season, putting up 98 points just a week earlier in Gampel.

Now, Creighton got what appeared to be an easy draw to win its first Big East tourney title. Only the Hoyas, who had finished in eighth place in the league standings at 7–9, suddenly decided to play like Ewing's dominant teams of the mid-1980s and rolled to a where-did-that-come-from 73–48 romp over the Bluejays.

Man, 2020–2021 was strange. "An irregular season," Hurley often called it.

For UConn, the job now was to flush the crushing loss behind and get ready for its first trip to the NCAA tournament in five years. This one would be played inside a "bubble" at sites in and around Indianapolis. Teams would be quarantined in downtown hotels except for practices and games, which would be played at places like Hinkle Fieldhouse in Indianapolis; Assembly Hall down in Bloomington, Indiana; and Mackey Arena, home of Purdue, out in West Lafayette.

And that's where UConn, the No. 7 seed in the East Regional, was pitted against 10th-seeded Maryland in an opening round game on March 20, 2021. Despite being the higher seed, the Terrapins turned out to be a terrible matchup for the Huskies.

And the staff knew it, immediately.

Maryland played a five-out, position-less type of ball that included constant switching on defense. It was something the Huskies struggled to handle against teams like Villanova and St. John's, and they struggled even more so against the Terps.

UConn dug a 14-point hole early in the second half, scrambled to get back within striking distance, but then bricked one foul shot after another down the stretch en route to a 63–54 loss.

The Huskies shot a mere 32 percent from the floor. They outrebounded Maryland 40–29, with many of those rebounds coming off their missed shots, but they failed to convert numerous putbacks.

Bouknight, in what wound up being his final game as a Husky, finished with 15 points on just 6-for-16 shooting.

Just like that, the "irregular season" was over. Yes, the Huskies had made their first NCAA tourney since 2016. The progress on the floor was evident.

But a first-round loss in the Big Dance doesn't really fly at UConn. In 18 trips to the NCAA tourney under Jim Calhoun, the Huskies only suffered two opening-round losses (in 2008 and 2012, the latter Calhoun's final season at the helm). Even Kevin Ollie never lost a first-round game, albeit in only two trips to the Big Dance in six seasons.

Isaiah Whaley, the senior forward, took a macro view of the season.

"I view it as a big step, especially for the program," he said on the postgame Zoom call. "I'm proud of everybody for sticking to it. We went through a lot this year, especially with the COVID pauses, everybody going through stuff individually. But we stuck through it and kept fighting. I see this as a big step for the program, and it's only up from here."

He was right.

Bouknight would soon become the program's 14th NBA lottery pick and first in nine seasons, selected No. 11 overall by Charlotte. And UConn was about to get some good news from one of its biggest recruits—literally and figuratively—in a long time.

8

Big Commitment

Adrian Wojnarowski, the ESPN basketball reporter whose "Woj Bombs" frequently broke big NBA news, had returned to his roots for a Q&A session with Dan Hurley at the Boys & Girls Club of Bristol on a wintry December 10, 2018.

Wojnarowski, a Bristol native, was very tight with the Hurley family, having written a book, *The Miracle of St. Anthony*, chronicling Bob Hurley Sr. and the Jersey City–based, powerhouse St. Anthony's basketball program.

After fielding about a half-hour of questions from Wojnarowski and about 150 fans and local businesspeople, Hurley signed autographs and took some selfies. One group of local basketball players wanted to get a picture with Hurley, but the coach had one stipulation: the big, nearly 7-foot-tall kid with the group couldn't be in the picture.

Hurley wasn't even familiar with the kid, just 15 at the time. But he couldn't risk taking a selfie with someone that he might someday recruit and risk some sort of NCAA violation.

Hurley and his staff were extremely sensitive to potential violations. Thanks to multiple violations incurred by Kevin Ollie over the prior couple of years, the program had been put on two years' probation in July 2019, losing a scholarship for the 2019–2020 season and incurring recruiting restrictions.

In fact, when assistant coach Tom Moore went to watch a recruit at the National Prep Showcase in New Haven that ensuing fall, he made sure he stepped out in the hallway when that recruit wasn't playing, so as not to go over the program's recruiting minutes limit.

And so, the big kid stepped aside as the rest of his teammates got a photo with Hurley.

That big kid was Donovan Clingan. He would end up taking plenty of photos with Hurley in the coming years.

Clingan was just a somewhat ungainly freshman at Bristol Central High School at the time. He would grow a few more inches, topping out at 7 feet 2 inches, and emerge as one of the most dominant players in Connecticut basketball history.

In 74 games over his career at Bristol Central, Clingan lost just 11 times—most of them as a freshman. He led the Rams to back-to-back, undefeated state championships as a junior and senior, frequently getting banged and brutalized by two or three defenders who were a foot shorter and draped all over him.

Perhaps the most surprising part about Clingan's high school career, however, was that he remained at Bristol Central, a public school in his hometown, for all four years. Typically, highly ranked prospects like Clingan, a consensus national top-75 recruit, transferred to a prep school by their sophomore or junior year, if not earlier. There, they'd play against better competition and get more exposure to high-major programs.

But Clingan was content to remain home. And there was good reason.

His mother, Stacey Porrini Clingan, was a star at Bristol Central three decades earlier, a 6-foot-4 center who set school records for career rebounds (1,032) and blocks (273). She went on to star at the University of Maine, where she scored 1,128 career points and was ultimately inducted into the school's athletics hall of fame.

Stacey died on March 27, 2018, at age 42 following a long bout with breast cancer. Donovan, just 14 at the time, wanted to carry on and honor her legacy.

At Bristol Central, he wore uniform No. 32, just like his mom, and set a goal of breaking her rebounding and blocked-shot records (he did). It was a truly beautiful, heartwarming story. In a town whose previous athletic hero, Aaron Hernandez, wound up bringing nothing but shame to the locals, Clingan was a great, 7-foot-2 source of community pride, a popular kid who could be seen with a camera around his neck, taking pictures at various Bristol Central sports events throughout his tenure, just like any other high schooler.

Still, playing in the Connecticut Interscholastic Athletic Conference, dominating a bunch of 6-foot-3 suburban centers, raised questions of how good Clingan really was. Could he withstand the rigors of the physical Big East after going against kids from Farmington and Glastonbury the prior four years? Why not prove himself against bigger and better competition at prep school?

Clingan wasn't worried, and neither was Dan Hurley. From the moment UConn began recruiting the 7-footer, Hurley was enamored with Clingan. For one, Clingan proved himself against top competition during the summer Amateur Athletic Union (AAU) circuit. More to the point, he showed a skill level and mobility rare for such a big man.

When it comes to in-state recruits, Hurley often bides his time. He wants to be extra sure that the kid is the right fit for his program, on several levels. Otherwise, it could all lead to an uncomfortable or embarrassing situation if the kid doesn't pan out, or if he spurned Hurley's advances for another program.

But by the end of Clingan's sophomore season, UConn offered him a scholarship. Ultimately, so did dozens of other schools, including the one Clingan grew up dreaming of playing for—Michigan, which happened to be coached by Juwan Howard, one of the stars of the program's fabled "Fab Five" team.

In the spring and summer of 2021, following a junior season in which he averaged 27.3 points and 17.2 rebounds, won a state championship, and was a Gatorade National Player of the Year finalist, Clingan made official visits to Michigan, Syracuse, and Ohio State. His final visit, on July 1, was UConn.

Most observers assumed Clingan would choose the hometown school, about 40 minutes from his Bristol home. But his father, Bill, insisted that he had no idea what his son would choose when he woke up on the second and final day of the visit, on July 2, in a Hartford hotel. Bill's biggest concern was that he had a work-related meeting later that morning (he'd make it).

Donovan Clingan told his dad that he was going to commit to UConn and do so later that day at a team barbecue at Hurley's Glastonbury home. They kept it a secret until then.

That evening, as Hurley tended to burgers and dogs on the backyard grill, Big Donovan called Hurley and assistant Tom Moore to the side.

Just like he had in high school, Donovan Clingan was staying home.

"We're signed up to help you get that fifth title," he told the coaches. "Let's get No. 5."

Little did anyone know how soon that would happen.

9
45:07

Donovan Clingan was still a year away from enrolling at UConn as the 2021–2022 season was on the horizon. But the Huskies' roster was already filling up with the type of high-level recruits that Hurley had envisioned for his program by Year 4.

Adama Sanogo, the ultra-skilled, 6-foot-9 center, and Andre Jackson Jr., a dynamic athlete and defender, were sophomores ready to take on bigger roles. Jordan Hawkins, a sweet-shooting, 6-foot-5 guard from Maryland's historic DeMatha Catholic program, enrolled at UConn that summer amid comparisons to Ray Allen. Samson Johnson, a wiry, 6-foot-10, rim-running athlete, had "wall potential" according to Hurley. That meant that someday, Johnson's banner could adorn the walls of the Werth Family Champions Center practice facility alongside former UConn NBA lottery picks like Allen, Richard Hamilton, Kemba Walker, and, most recently, James Bouknight.

In a prime example of the strangeness of the previous "COVID season," Hurley had never actually met Johnson in person until the Togo native arrived at campus that summer. In fact, almost all of UConn's (and every other school's) recruiting for the 2021 class was done by watching games on video or virtual workouts. No in-person meetings, not even on-campus visits, were allowed until the summer of 2021.

That led to a few recruiting misses for the Huskies. Still, UConn was recruiting at a high level, and that level got even higher after Hurley hired Luke Murray as an assistant to replace Kevin Freeman, who took on a different job in the UConn athletics department.

Murray had spent the previous six seasons as an assistant under head coach Chris Mack—three years at Xavier and three at Louisville. He was "blind-sided" when he and assistant Dino Guadio were not brought back to Mack's staff following the 2020–2021 season.

In swooped Hurley, who had a long history with Murray, hiring him as an assistant both at Wagner and Rhode Island. Murray was perhaps best known as the son of legendary actor/comedian Bill Murray. The *Caddyshack*, *Groundhog Day*, and *Ghostbusters* star would be a frequent face at UConn games in the ensuing years, just as he had been at Louisville and Xavier and Rhode Island (and Cubs' games and Bears' games and . . .).

But Luke Murray didn't want to live in his dad's shadow, preferring to make a name of his own. In college basketball circles, he was perhaps best known as a dynamic recruiter.

"It's been a love of mine," Murray told reporters shortly after being hired. "I'm blessed to be able to do it as a profession."

Murray was a student at UConn for a semester some 20 years earlier and remembered poking around the basketball offices with his buddy, team manager Mark Daigneault (the future head coach of the Oklahoma City Thunder), and kicking around names of recruits with assistant coaches Tom Moore and Andre LaFleur.

Murray soon transferred to Fairfield, about 90 minutes down the road. Upon graduation in 2007, he called Moore to congratulate him on recently landing the head coaching job at Quinnipiac. Moore asked if he could bounce a few recruits' names off Murray, and that eventually led to his first job as Quinnipiac's director of basketball operations.

Murray went on to numerous other assistant coaching jobs over the next decade or so before landing back with Hurley and alongside his other former boss, Moore.

Hurley was already establishing a recruiting and developmental program among the best in the nation. Look no further than Bouknight, who arrived in Storrs rated as the No. 53 recruit in the nation by the

247Sports rating service and left two years later as the No. 11 overall pick in the NBA Draft.

The future was looking brighter and brighter in Storrs. But heading into the 2021–2022 season, Dan Hurley was harking back to the recent past for motivation.

Hurley, as he does, had a mantra: "45:07."

What did it mean? It was a reference to the final 45 minutes, 7 seconds of UConn's 2020–2021 season. The final 5:07 of the Big East tournament semifinal loss to Creighton, when a five-point lead turned into a crushing three-point loss. And the 40 minutes of UConn's unsightly NCAA tourney loss to Maryland.

Hurley had that infamous time stamp—45:07—programmed on the scoreboards inside the practice facility, as a screen-saver on players' laptops. He even had T-shirts made with "45:07" emblazoned on the front, which he showed off to the media in June at the program's first in-person media availability in 18 months.

"You need things that are driving you," he explained. "You get at these guys in a (weight-lifting session) and somebody doesn't want to finish their last set on the bench, somebody's got to be in there yelling, '45:07!' You don't want to watch film as a coach on July 3 at 6 p.m. because you want to go food shopping for a barbecue the next day? 45:07. You need that to drive you."

UConn entered the 2021–2022 season ranked No. 24 in the land. It was the first time the Huskies began a season ranked since 2016, when they were No. 18—before dropping their first two home games to Wagner and Northeastern, a pair of low-majors and, ironically, the schools at which Kevin Ollie's successor (Hurley) and predecessor (Calhoun) had begun their respective college coaching careers.

No such home upsets happened this time around, as the Huskies dispatched their first four opponents with ease before hopping on a plane to the Bahamas to take part in the ultracompetitive Battle 4 Atlantis.

The Huskies opened up against No. 19 Auburn and, though the calendar had yet to flip to Thanksgiving, proceeded to stage what may have ended up being the best game of the entire college basketball season.

Adama Sanogo had a bit of a coming-out party, scoring 30 points around, through, and even over Auburn 7-footer Walker Kessler. Tyler Polley poured in a career-high 24 points off the bench, including a key bucket to spur a decisive 9–0 run late in the game. Jordan Hawkins, just a freshman, scored 16 points in 15 minutes, also off the bench.

The Huskies prevailed 115–109 in a double-overtime classic, the first two-overtime game in the event's history. There were 10 lead changes and eight ties throughout. When it was finally over, Isaiah Whaley fainted on the sidelines (he was fine).

The following day, UConn took on Michigan State and Hall of Fame coach Tom Izzo, a frequent opponent of the Huskies in non-league games over the prior 15 years. This wasn't a vintage Spartan team, but they jumped out to an early 14-point lead as UConn clearly looked tired from the day before. The Huskies battled back and owned a 55–48 lead with 4:44 to play.

This time, Michigan State authored the comeback and emerged with a 64–60 victory. The Huskies beat Virginia Commonwealth University (VCU) the following day 70–63 in an overtime slogfest, the exact opposite of the Auburn game two days earlier.

All told, it was a good enough showing for UConn, though as Hurley mentioned before leaving the Bahamas, "UConn comes to tournaments and expects to be playing for championships."

The Huskies' season marched on. They were ranked as high as No. 15 at one point and fell out of the rankings at another. There was a road loss at West Virginia in a Big East/Big 12 Battle, followed a few days later by a 10-point win over a good St. Bonaventure team in the Never Forget Tribute Classic in Newark, New Jersey, just around the corner from where Hurley's coaching career had begun at St. Benedict's Prep.

In their first Big East game before fans since that overtime win over Providence in March 2013, the Huskies fell to the Friars before a sellout crowd at Hartford's XL Center without Sanogo, who was injured. With Sanogo back in a limited role, they quickly rebounded with a tough win at Marquette, probably the best road win of Hurley's UConn career to that point.

There were a few more COVID postponements, but only one (a slated January 15 rematch at Providence) was never rescheduled.

And there were more losses to Villanova. The Huskies' record against 'Nova, still the standard-bearer of the Big East, had fallen to 0–4 under Hurley following an 85–74 loss at Wells Fargo Center on February 5. It's coming? It hadn't arrived quite yet.

But when eighth-ranked Villanova strode into XL Center a couple of weeks later for a rematch, Hurley and the Huskies had another chance to get over the hump.

10

"Huge Win for the Program"

UConn is one of the few basketball programs in the country that splits its home games between two venues: the 10,299-seat Gampel Pavilion on campus and the more than 16,000-seat XL Center in downtown Hartford.

Dan Hurley has always preferred playing home games—particularly big home games—at Gampel (at least when the roof isn't leaking). With a large student presence and smaller, more intimate setting, the domed arena can house one of the loudest, best atmospheres in college basketball.

Conversely, the XL Center, a former shopping mall that is also home to the minor-league hockey Hartford Wolfpack, can be a cavernous, cold building, with the ice always just below the hoops' hardwood floor. The old building, whose roof actually collapsed during the blizzard of 1978, could feel antiquated and empty if it wasn't packed with fans.

But when it was sold out for a big game, XL Center could get about as loud as any arena in the country. And that's the way it was when Villanova came to town on February 22, 2022, to face No. 21 UConn, which had won three straight and could all but assure itself of an NCAA tournament at-large bid with a win.

The sellout crowd was ready, rowdy, and riled up. And so was Hurley. Perhaps a bit too much.

Late in the first half, with Villanova up by a point, UConn's Tyrese Martin drove the lane but missed the layup. Hurley thought Martin had been fouled on the play and pounded the scorer's table in frustration.

He got hit with a technical foul. Fair enough.

But when 'Nova leading scorer Collin Gillespie stepped to the line to shoot the technical free throws, Hurley turned around to the crowd and wildly waved his arms up and down, prompting the fans to get noisy. One of the officials, veteran James Breeding, took exception to Hurley's overt actions and T'd him up again.

Hurley's second "T" meant he was ejected from the game.

"It was surreal," he'd say afterward. "I was stunned."

So was the sellout crowd, which booed vociferously, starting a "Refs, you suck!" chant that continued periodically the rest of the game.

Hurley eventually walked off the court, seemingly dejected. He watched the rest of the game on TV in the home locker room.

And he watched a classic.

Kimani Young took over head coaching duties. Young was hired as an assistant coach shortly after Hurley took over at UConn in April 2018. In September 2020, he was promoted to associate head coach.

Known as a great recruiter, he had brought in James Bouknight, Adama Sanogo, and Samson Johnson, among others. He had served as a coach, as well as athletic director, mentor, and other roles, in two separate stints with the New Height Youth Inc. program in New York City. He was an assistant coach for Rick Pitino's son, Richard, at both Florida International and Minnesota.

But he had never been a head coach in a college game before. Until now. In front of 15,564 fans. Against the No. 8 team in the country.

You would have never guessed it was Young's college head-coaching debut. Following Hurley's ejection, Young was the picture of poise on the sidelines. Hands on hips, calmly yet forcibly shouting out instructions, calling plays, even barking at the refs (though certainly not as vociferously as Hurley). He truly looked the part.

"Throughout my whole career," Hurley would say later, "I've always been smart enough to insulate myself with head coach-quality assistant coaches. Kimani is one of the best I've ever had with me."

Still, the Huskies appeared to be heading for their sixth straight loss to Villanova when they trailed by four points with 46.8 seconds left. Villanova's Caleb Daniels missed the front end of a one-and-one, however, and Tyler Polley nailed a 3-pointer with 20 seconds remaining.

Gillespie got tied up in the corner by R. J. Cole and Andre Jackson Jr. under UConn's full-court press and turned the ball over with 17.5 ticks remaining. After a UConn time-out, Cole, a lefty, hit a tough, right-handed runner to put the Huskies ahead for good.

Cole then capped an improbable comeback victory by drawing a charge on Gillespie in the final second.

"That's a winning play," said Young, who joined Hurley for the postgame press conference. "He's been doing that all year."

Indeed, it was the 19th charge Cole had taken on the season.

UConn had finally slayed Villanova, for the first time since rejoining the Big East. Dan Hurley had finally gotten that Jay Wright monkey off his back. That the win came with Hurley watching on TV in the locker room didn't seem to matter to the head coach.

"Just a huge win for the program," he said afterward.

UConn sandwiched wins over lowly Georgetown and DePaul around its fifth straight loss to Creighton, heading into the Big East tournament. The Huskies had fallen short of a coveted league regular-season title, but Hurley was intent on erasing the bad memory from the previous year's loss to Creighton and winning the league tourney title at Madison Square Garden. This time, in front of fans. Lots of fans.

First up, Seton Hall, Hurley's alma mater. No sweat, a 10-point victory. That brought up—you guessed it—Villanova, at a sold-out MSG on Friday night of the Big East tournament, one of the great environments in all of college sports.

This one was a back-and-forth battle with seven ties and a whopping 15 lead changes. Villanova led by eight with about 10 minutes left, but the Huskies got back to within two (62–60) with 10 seconds remaining.

Gillespie hit one of two free throws with 3 seconds left, and UConn wasn't able to get off a game-tying shot.

Villanova had won. Again. Even just a few weeks after the Huskies had finally exorcised some demons with that comeback win in Hartford.

The Wildcats beat Creighton the following night for the tournament title. They had won what UConn and Hurley so clearly coveted. Again.

Hurley would later admit that he didn't handle the loss well. He and the team scoured over video the following day in New York City before heading back to Storrs for CBS's Selection Sunday show. The loss stung, but there were still big goals at hand.

UConn's name popped up on the TV screen early that Sunday evening. And when the Huskies' opening-round opponent, New Mexico State, appeared seconds later, Hurley seemed to nod his head approvingly, perhaps anticipating an easier first-round matchup than Maryland a year earlier.

UConn was the No. 5 seed in the West Region, its highest seed since it was No. 3 in that 2011 championship campaign. The Huskies had a date with 12th-seeded New Mexico State up in Buffalo, where plenty of UConn fans would no doubt travel. Hurley's nodding approval seemed justified.

Not quite.

New Mexico State was led by a kid named Teddy Allen. Not a kid, really. Allen was 23 years old and on his fifth program in five years. You read that correctly. He played at West Virginia as a freshman, transferred to Wichita State but never played for the Shockers after being dismissed from the team following an arrest for suspicion of domestic violence. He played a year at Western Nebraska Community College, led Nebraska in scoring as a redshirt junior, and then transferred to New Mexico State University (NMSU) as a grad transfer.

He had a spotty past but plenty of talent. Allen led the Western Athletic Conference in scoring at 19.6 points per game. New Mexico State wasn't necessarily a one-man show, but it was clear that the 6-foot-5 guard was the one player the Huskies couldn't let beat them in their tourney-opener on March 17, 2022, at Buffalo's KeyBank Center.

And that's exactly what they let happen.

11

Buffaloed in Buffalo

It started innocently enough. With Andre Jackson Jr., UConn's long-armed, 6-foot-6 defensive stopper, guarding him all over the floor, Teddy Allen missed his first six shots.

Then, mostly with Jackson on the bench after picking up his second foul, Allen made his next five.

"He's going to make tough 2s!" Hurley shouted to his bench at one point late in the half.

Allen hit more than just "tough 2s." He hit long 3-pointers, some of which Hurley would later call "unguardable."

Allen hit a jumper with 39 seconds left in the half to give New Mexico State a 32–22 lead at the break. UConn was just 2-for-11 from three-point land and, worse, getting outrebounded by the Aggies 17–11.

The Huskies battled back in the latter half, led by R. J. Cole, who finished with a team-high 20 points. When Isaiah Whaley scored with 2:07 left in regulation, UConn had tied the game at 58.

NMSU's Will McNair missed a 3-pointer, but Clayton Henry grabbed the rebound and found Allen, who hit a 3-pointer.

Cole scored on a driving layup, but Allen was fouled with 52.4 seconds left and made both free throws. After a UConn turnover, Allen scored on a transition layup while being fouled and converted the free throw, putting the Aggies up six.

Tyrese Martin hit a corner 3-pointer with 18.9 seconds remaining, but Allen made four free throws over the final 17 seconds to seal New Mexico State's 70–63 victory.

It wasn't all Allen. The Aggies, who shot just 32.8 percent from the three-point line for the season, hit 11 of 17 (64.7 percent) against UConn. Henry, Sir'Jabari Rice, Johnny McCants, and Mike Peake combined to go 7-for-10 from distance. The Aggies outrebounded UConn 26–25, including eight on the offensive end—all eight seemingly coming at crucial times.

But . . . well, it was mostly Allen. He personally outscored the Huskies 15–9 over the final 4 minutes of play and finished with 37 points. He was 10-for-24 from the floor and made all 13 of his free throws.

"We wanted him to take tough shots, but he just happened to make more tough shots than he's used to," Martin said. "That's a credit to him."

New Mexico State had immediately become a dirty word among UConn fans. Perhaps not quite up there with George Mason, the No. 11 seed who knocked off the top-seeded, seemingly championship-bound Huskies in the 2006 Elite Eight. But close.

And Teddy Allen's name immediately moved up to the top of the list of UConn villains, alongside Marquette's Steve Novak (41 points in UConn's Big East opener in 2005), Gerry McNamara (who led Syracuse to a rousing 2006 Big East tourney title, with UConn the first victim), and others.

But all that was secondary.

The real story was that UConn had been bounced from the first round of the NCAA tournament for a *second* straight year. And that's something that just doesn't happen at UConn. In fact, it had never happened in 18 seasons under Jim Calhoun.

Now, Calhoun didn't always get to the NCAA tourney. The Huskies fell into a pattern of serious runs at national titles dotted every few years with a trip to the National Invitational Tournament (or, in 2006–2007, no postseason at all).

Calhoun got bounced from the first round at UConn just twice, in 2008 and 2012. He followed the first one with a trip to the Final Four. After the second one, he retired.

Hurley had guided UConn back from three straight losing seasons for the first time in more than 30 years to consecutive NCAA tourney bids for the first time in a decade. But first-round losses to lower-seeded opponents (New Mexico State? Really?) had marred his otherwise impressive program turnaround.

Hurley was already starting to feel the pressure. He and his team nearly left KeyBank Center before meeting with the media after Hurley and a couple of players had to stand outside in the hallway while New Mexico State's postgame press conference ran late.

Hurley ultimately convened inside the press room and said all the right things. He gave New Mexico State and Teddy Allen credit. He was legitimately hurt that guys like R. J. Cole, Isaiah Whaley, and Tyler Polley, all of whom had helped the program's rebirth, had played their final games as Huskies.

"It's crushing," Hurley said. "Just wish we had an opportunity to coach these guys longer. It's a special group, a great group. They've done so much for UConn these last couple of years. It's just sad."

But Hurley knew things had to change. He knew this couldn't happen again. And this was something that wasn't going to be solved by a slogan or catchphrase. No "45:07" T-shirts this time around.

Hurley knew he had to recruit different players. Guys like Whaley and Polley (who he inherited from Kevin Ollie) and Cole and Tyrese Martin (who he took in as transfers) were tough and gritty. But they weren't the type of dynamic athletes that led teams to national championships.

More to the point, they weren't shooters. Not great ones, anyway. And after watching his Huskies shoot exactly 7-for-23 on 3-pointers in two straight first-round NCAA losses, Hurley knew he had to bring in some bona fide marksmen to the program.

For all his dynamic athleticism, deft passing, and defensive prowess, Andre Jackson Jr. was a huge liability from long distance. Adama Sanogo had displayed some shooting range as a sophomore but was still primarily a back-to-the-basket big man. And Hurley had no intentions of letting Donovan Clingan ever take a shot from beyond the 3-point arc.

But Hurley already had a few shooters in stock. Jordan Hawkins had just completed an up-and-down freshman season. He scored a season-high 16 points in that double-overtime classic win over Auburn in the Bahamas, but he seemed to battle self-confidence (and injuries) for much of the rest of the season. Ultimately, he missed UConn's final four games while in concussion protocol.

Alex Karaban, a 6-foot-8 shooter from nearby Southborough, Massachusetts, had enrolled at UConn for the second semester after an accelerated graduation from IMG Academy. He sat out the second half of the season as a redshirt, but he earned valuable practice time with the team and was expected to be a key contributor in 2022–2023.

The Huskies brought in Tristen Newton, a transfer from East Carolina University. Newton wasn't a great long-distance shooter, but he was a 6-foot-5 guard who was "wired to score," per his former ECU coach, Joe Dooley. He was also familiar to Hurley, having poured in 25 points in a loss to the Huskies late in that ill-fated, 2019–2020 season, a game better remembered for James Bouknight's otherworldly, one-handed alley-oop dunk.

Newton averaged 17.7 points per game as a junior in the relative anonymity of ECU. Over his next two seasons at UConn, he would emerge as one of the best, and winningest, players in program history, establishing a program record with four triple-doubles.

Also off the transfer market, Hurley brought in guards Nahiem Alleyne from Virginia Tech and Hassan Diarra from Texas A&M. Diarra was the all-time leading scorer at Putnam Science Academy, the top-notch prep program about a half-hour northeast of UConn's campus. He was the brother of UConn director of player development Mamadou Diarra, whose playing career with the Huskies had been cut short a couple of years earlier due to chronic knee issues. And he had the clutch gene, hitting two game-winning, buzzer-beating 3-pointers the prior season at A&M.

Then there was Joey Calcaterra, perhaps the least-heralded of the Huskies' multiple newcomers. The 6-foot-3 guard from out near San

Francisco had spent his first four years of college at San Diego, a good but not great shooter in the good-but-not-great West Coast Conference.

He would leave UConn roughly 10 months later as one of the most beloved one-and-done Huskies in program history . . . along with perhaps the program's greatest nickname: Joey California.

Sad Story of Akok Akok

Dan Hurley and his staff have largely hit on their most coveted recruits. And when those recruits reach campus, they have been able to stay healthy, for the most part, and lead the Huskies to great success.

Then there's the sad story of Akok Akok. A wiry, 6-foot-9 forward who was born in Sudan but lived almost all his life in Manchester, New Hampshire, Akok was one of Hurley's first major recruits, a national top-25 prospect coming out of nearby Putnam Science Academy. He joined the program in the second semester of 2019 but didn't play, only practiced, as Alex Karaban would do a few years later.

As a redshirt freshman, Akok led the AAC in blocked shots at 2.6 per game. More notably, he won over UConn fans with his hustle—sprinting up the court like Usain Bolt while others jogged—his youthful exuberance, and megawatt smile.

It all came to a crashing halt on February 16, 2020, inside the first few minutes of a key showdown with Memphis at XL Center. Akok swatted away Memphis big man Precious Achiuwa's shot 56 seconds into the game, then came down on his left leg, immediately started hopping around, and ultimately crumbling to the floor in pain.

He tried to get up but couldn't, his face a study in pain and anguish. He knew.

Torn Achilles tendon. A potential career-killer for a basketball player.

In typical Akok fashion, he remained on the bench for the remainder of the game, even as UConn's medical staff suggested he go to a nearby hospital for an MRI. That could wait. He wanted to see his team win. And win UConn did.

"Just seeing him out there says a lot about him," junior center Josh Carlton said. "Akok loves his team, loves the game of basketball."

Dan Hurley could barely contain his tears in the postgame press conference. "Sports is brutal sometimes," he said. "Life is brutal sometimes."

Akok Akok's sports career, and his life, would never be the same.

He endured a grueling, repetitive, "boring" (in his words) offseason rehab regimen, made more difficult through the COVID-19 pandemic, and was eager to return to the Huskies' rotation the following season. He did, even scoring 7 points in 10 minutes off the bench in a mid-February win at Xavier. But it was clear he returned too early; he played only three more games during the rest of the season.

Akok was back in the rotation in 2021–2022, starting seven games and notching a few double-figure scoring outputs. But with freshman Adama Sanogo emerging as a star and veteran Isaiah Whaley establishing himself as the ultimate "glue guy," Akok's minutes started to diminish. He played just 2 minutes in the season-ending loss to New Mexico State.

He soon entered the transfer portal, did lunch with West Virginia Hall of Fame coach Bob Huggins right outside UConn's campus, and ultimately enrolled at Big East rival Georgetown.

"Some exit conversations are brief and some are emotional," Hurley told reporters at the time. "That was emotional for me. His growth as a young man, from when he stepped on campus, was just amazing in terms of growth as a person, how much more mature and prepared he is going into the next part of his career. That one hit me."

When the Hoyas visited Gampel Pavilion on December 20, 2022, Akok had to be the first Georgetown player ever to receive a loud ovation from Husky fans. He played one season with the Hoyas, starting all 31 games and averaging 6.5 points and 2.0 blocks per game. He transferred the next season to West Virginia, where Huggins no longer coached. During a preseason exhibition game, Akok collapsed to the floor and was rushed to the hospital. He would return to action a little over a month later and *wound up playing in 23 games for the Mountaineers, averaging 3 points per contest.*

And that was it. A heart issue prevented Akok from extending his playing career any further. A basketball career, which had started with so much promise, had come to a rather sad end.

12

Portland Trail-blazing

Dan Hurley didn't necessarily have to win an NCAA tournament championship in 2022–2023. But he certainly needed to win an NCAA tournament *game*. Or else—no, he wouldn't be fired, or even on the hot seat. Not even close. But a third straight first-round ouster from the Big Dance would gin up a fan base spoiled by four national titles over the prior 24 years. He'd hear it at the corner stores and supermarkets and, more to the point, on message boards and social media.

And he knew it.

"I've got to find a way to get the program over the hump, to go from contending to a championship team in our league," he told *CT Insider* in October 2022. "And I've got to go from a team that's having a really strong, successful regular season to getting on a run in March."

He insisted it wasn't something he thought about or stressed over much. But when asked if the pressure and expectations would be ramped up if (when?) the Huskies heard their name on Selection Sunday five months later, he confessed: "It may creep in at that point—or, let me change that—it'll *definitely* creep in at that point. Not being successful is something, from the psychological standpoint, we as coaches are going to be keenly aware of. That push-and-pull, where you're going into that moment: 'Do I keep it too loose, because I'm worried about the team being too tight? Am I afraid that my team's not going to be as intense?'

"It'll definitely be going through my mind," Hurley continued, "maybe in the middle of the night when I wake up."

At URI, Hurley had posted first-round tourney wins over Creighton in 2017 and Oklahoma in 2018. But there was a "looseness," he noted, of being the underdog. That doesn't really happen at UConn.

"When we get back to that moment, I think it's something the coaching staff will carry," Hurley continued. "But I think that this team is so different. . . . I think it'll be the burden for me to carry, and rightfully so. That's the beauty of having such a new team. If we can put ourselves back in that position, I don't think they'll be wearing it."

About a week later, at Big East Media Day at Madison Square Garden, the league's coaches chose Adama Sanogo as preseason Player of the Year, which was nice. But Big East coaches predicted the Huskies would finish fourth in the 11-team league, behind (in order) Creighton, Xavier, and Villanova.

UConn also entered the season unranked in both the Associated Press and *USA Today* coaches' polls. Hurley would later note that "nobody" ranked the Huskies in the preseason, which was and wasn't true. No, the team wasn't ranked in either of the major polls, but it's not like none of the writers (including yours truly) or coaches voted for them. UConn was just two spots out of the AP Top 25 and four out of the coaches' poll. But Hurley never had to look far to find disrespect.

The Huskies opened the season with five wins over a collection of cupcake opponents, all by 20 points or more, all but one by at least 30 points. They had entered the rankings at No. 20 by the time they flew out to Portland, Oregon, for the Phil Knight Invitational.

UConn shared a flight to the Thanksgiving-week tournament with the UConn women's team, which was a rarity. The last time the two programs had shared a chartered flight had been 27 years earlier, on January 28, 1995, for a doubleheader with the Kansas men's and women's teams at Kemper Arena in Kansas City.

It didn't go so well for Jim Calhoun's troops.

The No. 1–ranked UConn women, ultimately en route to the first of their 12 national titles, topped Kansas 97–87. The No. 2–ranked men's squad got blitzed by 29 points by the ninth-ranked Jayhawks.

If the flight out to Kansas City was already a bit awkward, given the icy relationship between Calhoun and women's coach Geno Auriemma, the flight home was downright freezing.

"I was in a bad mood, the kids, because of me, were in a bad mood," Calhoun recalled. "One team celebrated, and the other team was . . . not in a great mood."

In fact, the women's team's celebration was largely muted on the flight home, with Auriemma sitting quietly at the back of the plane.

"They won, we lost, and I honestly didn't have a great time on the plane," Calhoun continued. "We had conflicting viewpoints on the world at that particular point. I don't mean the women and men, I just mean how the game turned out and how each team felt about itself."

"It could have been worse," the coach added. "It could have been a five-hour bus trip. I've been through worse things in my life."

Calhoun and Auriemma never really got along, for a variety of reasons: Calhoun is 12 years older than Auriemma and was never really willing to cede the spotlight to the women's coach. Auriemma wasn't exactly enamored by the way Calhoun composed himself at times, including some occasional barbs thrown at Auriemma's program and older fan base.

But Hurley and Auriemma got along beautifully from the start. They sat across the aisle from each other on the six-and-a-half-hour, 757 flight from Hartford to Portland and engaged in some "interesting conversations" that went to "a lot of places," per Auriemma.

Then, when it came to the basketball, both teams went out and dominated.

The women beat Duke and Iowa to win the smaller, Phil Knight Legacy title. That was to be somewhat expected of the No. 3–ranked Huskies.

What the men's team did was far more remarkable. The Huskies opened up against the "host" school, Oregon, which also happens to be the alma mater of Phil Knight, whose 85th birthday the tournament celebrated. With Knight watching from courtside, UConn totally dismantled the Ducks 83–59 on Thanksgiving night. The Huskies hit a school-record 17 three-pointers, led by five apiece from Tristen Newton

(23 points) and Jordan Hawkins (18) and three off the bench from Joey Calcaterra, who was by now sporting the Hurley-invented nickname "Joey California."

The next day, the Huskies faced a powerful, 18th-ranked Alabama squad coached by Nate Oats, a close friend of the Hurley family who was an assistant for Dan's older brother, Bobby, at Buffalo.

No sweat. The Huskies broke open a 52–52 game with a head-spinning, 16–1 run and cruised to an 82–67 triumph behind 25 points from Adama Sanogo and 16 from Hawkins.

After a day off, UConn kept the pedal to the metal in the championship game against Iowa State. This one wasn't as pretty, more of a defensive slugfest, but the Huskies won in equally dominant fashion, 71–53.

Hurley, who as a motivational tool places poster board cutouts of each championship trophy the Huskies can win each season in practices, was ecstatic.

"This was the first of four chances [to win a title], so I'm happy we got one," the coach said, before adding with dramatic effect, "so far."

Indeed, the Big East regular-season and tournament titles, and, of course, the NCAA tournament title, all remained in the Huskies' sights.

Andre Jackson Jr., just returned from an injury that kept him out of the Huskies' first five games, had 10 points, 13 rebounds, and 5 assists off the bench. Newton added 13 points and Alex Karaban 10, and Joey California provided instant offense off the bench for the third straight game.

But it was Donovan Clingan who was the star of this show, taking over for a struggling, foul-plagued Sanogo and scoring a team-high 15 points to go with 10 rebounds in just 18 minutes off the bench.

The 7-foot-2 freshman was named the tournament's Most Outstanding Player. Perhaps there was no better example of UConn's superior depth than the fact that the team's backup center, who only averaged about 13 minutes per game, was named Most Outstanding Player in a prestigious tournament title.

The beat went on for the Huskies, who suddenly found themselves ranked No. 8 in the country. UConn's complex offense, masterminded by Hurley and Luke Murray, was clicking on all cylinders. There was a

10-point win over Oklahoma State in a Big East/Big 12 Battle game at Gampel, after which Cowboy coach Mike Boynton proclaimed: "I don't know if [No.] 8 is high enough for this team. I've watched them play every one of their games, and I saw a team that, from my view, for whatever it's worth, can win a national championship."

The Huskies went down to Florida and dismantled the Gators by 21 points. They won their first three Big East games over Butler, Georgetown, and Villanova, to improve to 14–0 overall. UConn had ascended to No. 2 in the nation, behind only Purdue, by the time it headed out to Cincinnati for a New Year's Eve 2022 bout with 22nd-ranked Xavier.

Then, things hit a bit of a snag.

13

January of Discontent

January is often the coldest month of the year and, with 31 days, can seem like the longest. But that isn't why the month had become a dirty word in UConn basketball circles, right along with "George Mason" and "Teddy Allen," by the time the 2023 version was over.

The high-flying Huskies, who looked so deep, talented and dominant in Portland and had gone from unranked to No. 2 in the nation, nearly went back to unranked by the end of January. In fact, "January" would soon take on multiple parts of speech in Hurley's vocabulary: noun ("I hate January"), verb ("We got January-ed"), adjective ("That was a January performance") and, above all, expletive.

It actually began on December 31, 2022, with that afternoon game at Xavier. With 2:25 left and UConn trailing by two, Tristen Newton was called for a foul on Xavier's Zach Freemantle. Freemantle hit the first foul shot, but Hurley continued voicing his displeasure with the call. While he claimed he merely yelled, "Unbelievable!," he was hit with a technical.

Souley Boum hit both technical free throws, Freemantle returned to the line to hit his second, and suddenly Xavier's lead was six.

The Musketeers held on for the 83–73 win. Xavier wound up with a 28–9 advantage at the foul line. UConn committed 22 fouls, the Musketeers only 9. Asked whether, good call or bad call, he regretting picking up that key technical, Hurley replied: "Put yourself in my shoes.

You're aware of the free-throw discrepancy while the game is going on. You look at the first half and they've got one team foul through 15 or 16 minutes. So, you see that, that's factoring into your brain."

"Yes," Hurley concluded, "I wish I wouldn't have said 'Unbelievable.' But, put yourself in my shoes, when you factor in all those things."

Of course, one reason for the free-throw discrepancy was that the Huskies hoisted up a whopping 37 three-point attempts, the second most ever attempted in a game against Xavier. Driving to the basket gets you fouled, not firing up shots from long distance.

Either way, UConn's hopes for an undefeated season, however unreasonable, were over. Adama Sanogo admitted after the game that the team had harbored those dreams. That's the kind of confidence that had been pouring through the team.

UConn's hopes for a No. 1 ranking the following week were also shot. But this was just the beginning of their January of discontent.

On January 4, 2023, the now fourth-ranked Huskies made the hour-long bus ride to play their border rival, Providence, at the always-rowdy Dunkin' Donuts Center. Once again, an avalanche of referees' whistles hurt UConn, as the Friars nearly doubled the Huskies' free-throw attempts, 35–19. Bryce Hopkins, the Friars' talented transfer from Kentucky, exploited a defensive mismatch against freshman Alex Karaban and powered his way to 27 points. He shot nearly as many free throws (15) as UConn's entire team.

Hurley did his best to bite his tongue about the officiating after the game, but he was clearly peeved.

On January 7 at Gampel against Creighton, Hurley used a bit of his unique motivational skills to get the Huskies (briefly) back on track. The coach had unearthed a podcast recorded in the preseason in which Creighton center Ryan Kalkbrenner seemed to belittle the UConn program in general and Adama Sanogo in particular.

When asked during the podcast which opponent he most looks forward to playing, Kalkbrenner replied: "UConn, obviously. The teams have had a good rivalry, and obviously they've got Sanogo who they picked as player of the year. I've got to bite my tongue a little bit about my thoughts on that selection. But, definitely looking forward to that game and seeing what people think about player of the year after that."

UConn had never beaten the Bluejays in five games since rejoining the Big East in 2020–2021. When told that UConn fans had the Creighton game circled on their calendars, Kalkbrenner replied: "If I had never beaten a team and lost to them every single time I've played them, I'd circle that game, too. It's fun to go up against bigs that other people say are good. Me, I don't know about that. Last year, I did really, really [well] against them. I'm just looking to repeat that performance, because that would go a long way toward proving people wrong for that selection."

Hurley played the interview to the entire team, and they responded. Particularly Sanogo.

The 6-foot-9 junior forward scored 26 points on array of spin moves around, through, and even over the 7-foot-1 Kalkbrenner to lead UConn to a 69–60 win. He also grabbed 9 rebounds. Kalkbrenner finished with a nearly invisible 9 points and 4 boards in 33 minutes.

Sanogo sure had the game circled on his calendar.

"If you know me, I take stuff personally," he said. "So, for him to say stuff like that, coming into this game, I was ready to go."

"He did take it personally," Hurley noted. "For us, we don't want our players talking negatively about other teams or other programs. That bothered Adama. I think it bothered everyone. We don't want our guys to build a name for themselves by speaking negatively about others. I'm not gonna lie to you, we looked at the quote, we played the clip [Friday]."

UConn's two-game losing streak was over, but its January was far from finished. And it was about to get ugly. Real ugly.

Four days later, the Huskies squandered an 11-point lead and fell to Marquette 82–76 at Milwaukee's Fiserv Forum. Fair enough. Marquette was one of the Big East's best teams, and Fiserv a tough place for any team to win.

UConn returned home to face a middling St. John's team in Hartford on January 15. A good way to get back on track, right?

Wrong.

The game was a noon start on a Sunday, and the Huskies played as if they had been partying a little too much on Saturday night. The Huskies turned the ball over 21 times, turning into 22 Red Storm points. They allowed St. John's to drive to the basket at will while struggling mightily to score themselves, shooting just 4 for 17 from the three-point line.

Jordan Hawkins scored a career-high 31 points but also turned the ball over seven times. After that, not much to highlight for the Huskies. Andre Jackson Jr. finished with just 2 points. Donovan Clingan went scoreless in just 9 minutes off the bench. Mild-mannered Adama Sanogo was ejected in the final minute for cursing at the referees.

Then there was Tristen Newton, who played not only his worst game as a Husky but one of the worst games of his college career. Newton went scoreless in 18 minutes. He attempted just one shot, a 3-pointer, and two free throws, one of which he air-balled. He tried to hit Jackson with an alley-oop lob to start the second half, but it sailed about 15 feet over Jackson's head.

"Didn't see it coming," Hurley mused after the game. "We've become a team that's easy to beat."

Years later, Hurley still couldn't explain why the Huskies played so poorly on this day against a St. John's team that would fail to make even the NIT and fire head coach Mike Anderson when the season ended.

All of a sudden, the Huskies were .500 (4–4) in Big East play. And it would get worse.

Hurley tried to celebrate his 50th birthday the following day but couldn't. Especially when he took ill and tested positive for COVID-19. That would sideline him for a January 18 road game against his alma mater, Seton Hall. Typically, associate head coach Kimani Young would have taken over head coaching duties, but he contracted COVID as well. Neither Hurley nor Young made the trip to Newark, New Jersey.

That left the game in the hands of Luke Murray and Tom Moore. Murray essentially assumed head coaching duties and appeared to have the Huskies in good hands while Hurley could only watch on TV from his Glastonbury, Connecticut, home.

UConn led by as many as 17 points in the first half and owned a 14-point edge at halftime. But the Hall gradually clawed back and took its first lead of the game on a Kadary Richmond jumper with 1:12 remaining.

Tristen Newton's two free throws put UConn back on top 6 seconds later. With about 3 seconds left, Seton Hall's Femi Odukale front-rimmed a 3-point attempt, but the rebound fell straight into KC Ndefo's hands, and he put it back in and was fouled with 1.6 seconds left.

He missed the free throw, but UConn botched the rebound and had the most deflating of its five losses over its last six games.

The Huskies trailed for exactly 7 seconds the entire game. But that's all it took. They had now lost three straight games for the first time in three seasons.

"We're heartbroken," Newton said. "We should have won that one."

"I thought I did a poor job in the second half of coaching the guys, particularly offensively," said Murray.

But this wasn't Luke Murray's fault, or Tom Moore's, or Dan Hurley's, or any one particular person. This was a program-wide failing, a once-promising season seemingly coming apart at the seams.

The staff scrambled for answers. Play Donovan Clingan and Adama Sanogo together as a double-big-man combo? Play the struggling Newton less and Hassan Diarra or Nahiem Alleyne more? And what to do with Andre Jackson Jr., who contributed in so many areas except shooting, to the point where teams were "disrespectfully" slacking off on him defensively, practically begging him to shoot.

There were no easy answers.

A 30-point home romp over lowly Butler in Hartford brought some good feelings back, but then came a rematch with 13th-ranked Xavier in Gampel. The Musketeers jumped out to a 9–0 start and held leads of 20–9, 28–13, and 35–18 in the first half. They led by 16 with just under 17 minutes left before UConn (particularly Jordan Hawkins) caught fire.

Hawkins scored 26 of his game-high 28 points in the latter half, and UConn closed to within a single point four different times. But the Huskies could never get over the hump and lost, 82–79.

It snapped UConn's 17-game winning streak at Gampel that dated back to 2020–2021. It dropped the Huskies to 5–6 in the Big East. It was their sixth loss in their last eight games.

UConn would lose just six of its next 61 games over the ensuing nearly two-year span.

But there was no way of knowing that on January 25, 2023. The only thing that was sure was this: January was almost over. Just one more game, on January 31 at DePaul. The Huskies scored a 90–76 triumph over the Blue Demons, who would win just three of their 20 league games that season.

Whatever, a win was a win. January was over—but never forgotten.

"That was a leadership moment for me, in terms of how I deal with a team emotionally, and how I handle my own emotions," Hurley told *CT Insider* a couple of years later. "All these different points before your program breaks through and becomes a championship organization, whether it was tactics or leadership, you have these different moments where you have to look in the mirror and improve as a coach and as a leader. Those are the moments that make you. I was melting down in January.

"It's funny, these different moments," he continued. "They identify these different blind spots or vulnerabilities, or areas as a coach where you need to improve."

14

Back in Championship Form

On to February. The first day of the rest of the Huskies' lives was a good one, a 68–62 win at Georgetown on February 4, 2023. Granted, it took some late-game heroics from freshman Alex Karaban to put away the pesky, Patrick Ewing–coached Hoyas, who would finish the season 2–18 in the Big East. But it was a win.

UConn, which had never quite fallen out of the AP Top 25, hosted 10th-ranked Marquette on February 7 in Hartford and put on a clinic. The final score of 87–72 was hardly indicative of how thoroughly the Huskies dominated. They led by 20 points in the first half, 17 at halftime, and as much as 25 midway through the latter half. Tristen Newton finished with his second triple-double of the season—12 points, 10 rebounds, and 12 assists—to tie Shabazz Napier's program record for a career and set a new UConn mark for most triple-doubles in a single season.

"They played just like they were playing when they were 14–0 and No. 2 in the country," Marquette coach Shaka Smart marveled.

Indeed, later in the season, members of the coaching staff admitted that it was this February 7 win over Marquette that made them realize the Huskies were not only back but also capable of winning it all.

UConn was ready for a "revenge tour" against teams it had lost to in January. But first, there was a trip out to Omaha, where the team did what it always did—lose to Creighton. This one was closer, 56–53.

Jordan Hawkins hit what appeared to be a game-tying 3-pointer in the waning seconds, but replay review overturned it, revealing his toe on the line.

No worries. Over the ensuing week, the Huskies scored revenge wins over Seton Hall and Providence at home, then St. John's at Madison Square Garden. They crushed DePaul at home, then closed out their regular season in Philadelphia by completing a season series sweep of Villanova.

It's coming.

UConn was 24–7 overall. The Phil Knight Invitational trophy belonged to the Huskies, but the goal of winning their first Big East regular-season championship under Hurley was foiled by January. Marquette won the league title at 17–3. In fact, UConn wound up finishing in fourth place, just as the league coaches had predicted back in October, at 13–7—behind Marquette, Xavier, and Creighton and tied with Providence, with whom the Huskies would have a third date in a first-round Big East tournament game at Madison Square Garden.

Hurley still had two of those poster cutouts in full view during practices and meetings: the Big East tournament trophy and the NCAA tournament trophy. Both were still up for grabs. And while the latter was obviously any coach's ultimate goal, the former meant plenty to Hurley, Big East blood pumping through his veins.

Prior to UConn's March 9, 2023, meeting with the Friars, the Big East announced its individual-award winners, providing Hurley with a little more ammunition. Marquette's Tyler Kolek had beaten out Sanogo for Player of the Year. Sanogo and Jordan Hawkins each made first team All–Big East, but no one else (not Clingan, not Newton, not Karaban) made second team or honorable mention.

But what really irked Hurley was that Karaban had been beaten out by Villanova's Cam Whitmore for Freshman of the Year. Whitmore had better overall numbers and a better NBA future (he'd be a first-round draft pick a few months later). But Karaban was a more integral member of a much better team (Villanova wound up getting popped in the first round of the NIT, a game in which Whitmore didn't even play).

Whether disrespect or border rivalry or just feeling real good about themselves, the Huskies were fueled by something the next night against Providence as they jumped to an early lead, led 35–19 at halftime, and held onto the lead by as much as 26 with 12:30 left to play.

The Friars turned up the full-court pressure and managed to close to within as little as five with 3:33 remaining, capped by a layup by Corey Floyd Jr., who had transferred from UConn to Providence after sitting out the prior season at Storrs as a redshirt.

Hurley called a time-out, Hawkins knocked down a long 3-pointer, and the Huskies made it to the finish line with a 73–66 victory.

UConn, for the third straight season, had advanced to the Big East tournament semifinals, Friday night at Madison Square Garden, one of the truly magical settings of the New York sports scene. This time (unlike in 2021) fans were in attendance, a large number of them Husky fans in the building that the fan base frequently called "Storrs South."

"UConn owns this building," Hurley said after the win over Providence.

And this time, no Villanova standing in its way. Just Marquette. Yes, the league regular-season champs but a program that had never even been to the Big East tournament finals after some 20 seasons in the league.

No way the Golden Eagles were going to stand in the way of a Big East tournament title Hurley and the Huskies wanted so badly. Right?

Well . . .

Marquette caught the Huskies off guard by jumping them with ball pressure early in the game, putting UConn on its heels. Karaban's 3-pointer made it a 38–38 tie at halftime, but Marquette hit its first six shots of the latter half and opened its lead to as much as 10.

UConn went to an expansive zone defense that was effective, allowing it to tie the game at 60 on a Joey Calcaterra pull-up 3-pointer. But the Huskies could not quite get over the hump, never leading in the second half.

With 2:37 to play, Adama Sanogo scored on an inside hoop to get UConn to within three. Shockingly, those were the final points of the game, by either team. With 39 seconds left, Calcaterra had a wide-open look for a 3-pointer from the corner.

"I thought it was going in," he later explained. "It just hit the back rim."

UConn had one last chance but failed to use its last time-out and settled for an off-balance Hawkins 3-ball that missed badly.

"Disappointing loss," Hurley said afterward.

Rather satisfactory for Shaka Smart, however.

"It felt like a lot of people were giving UConn the game coming in," the Marquette coach noted. "And there were comments made about who owns the Garden and that kind of stuff. And, you know, we said, 'Wait a minute, we won this league.' So, we're not taking a back seat to anybody."

Marquette would win its first Big East tourney title the following night against Creighton. The Golden Eagles were Big East regular-season and tourney champions, two goals UConn aimed for at season's start.

But there was one more big goal still left. The biggest one of all. And this time, after a third straight Big East tournament semifinal loss, Hurley was going to handle things differently.

Rather than stew over game film over the next couple of days, as he had the previous year, Hurley immediately put the Marquette loss in the rear-view mirror. He had learned from the prior season that the disappointment of the Big East tourney loss to Villanova may have bled into the first-round NCAA tourney loss to New Mexico State. He freely admitted his team was too tight heading into that game, blaming himself as well as his basketball operations staff for not creating the right atmosphere.

"There were things that we didn't do to get our team excited about the opportunity to advance in the tournament," he recalled.

This time, Hurley was going to adapt. And that seemed evident on Selection Sunday inside the Werth Family Champions Center, where Hurley seemed to be in a lighthearted, jubilant mood.

And that didn't change, even when the Selection Committee seemed to play a cruel joke on Hurley and the Huskies.

15

"Go Win a Championship"

UConn earned a No. 4 seed (fair enough) in the West Region, the region that had launched three of the Huskies' four prior national championship runs. And the Huskies were placed in the subregional in Albany, New York, which was not only Andre Jackson Jr.'s hometown but also a quick, three-hour drive or so for thousands of UConn fans to flood MVP Arena.

And UConn's first-round opponent? Iona. No big deal, right? Iona was a good program from the MAAC conference, which Connecticut-based Quinnipiac and Sacred Heart called home, but hardly a threat for a first-round upset—until you realized that the team was coached by Rick Pitino. That's Hall of Famer Rick Pitino, who won a pair of national titles at Kentucky and Louisville (even if the latter was since vacated due to multiple, sordid NCAA violations).

It was hard to believe there could have been a worse No. 13 seed for UConn to face than Iona and Pitino, who had somehow engineered Providence to a Final Four run in 1987 as a No. 6 seed and was arguably the greatest X's and O's coach of his generation. Especially for Hurley, so desperate to get that monkey off his back and avoid a third straight NCAA tourney first-round ouster.

There was worry heading into the game on March 17, 2023, even if it wasn't always articulated.

"There are things you know but you don't talk about, and it was there," assistant coach Tom Moore would say later. "It's been there since the New Mexico State game."

Some of those worries Hurley predicted he'd have back in October were starting to crop up.

"It was an unfathomable feeling," he noted.

Sure enough, Iona battled the Huskies hard over the first 20 minutes and owned a 39–37 lead at halftime. Jordan Hawkins, the team's second-leading scorer, was 0-for-6 from the floor, on the heels of a 2-for-11 clunker a week earlier against Marquette.

At halftime, Hurley put on a master class of both serenity and strategy, showing how much he had improved and matured as a coach since the days of being ejected from a closed-door scrimmage.

"It's a long halftime," Tom Moore recalled. "He came in [the locker room], hit the team with a quick message, very supportive, very calm. He came in with [the coaching staff], spent five, six, seven minutes with us, and we were more rattled than he was. He was very calm, very calculated, thinking things through, taking our ideas and sorting out his ideas."

Then, Hurley went back out to face his players for the final six or seven minutes of the break.

"It was very calming, very soothing, very assuring," Moore reported. "And they came out in the second half and played that way."

UConn designed a play it hadn't run all year for Hawkins to curl off a screen for a 3-pointer on its first possession of the latter half. He connected, got fouled and hit the free throw.

"When you see the first one go in," Hawkins said later, "it's always a relief."

Adama Sanogo dunked home a lob from Andre Jackson Jr., Hawkins hit another trey, and Pitino called time-out.

UConn never looked back, never trailed again, as Sanogo poured in 22 of his game-high, season-high 28 points in the latter half and Hawkins added 13 en route to an 87–63 win.

Afterward, Hurley and Pitino met briefly in the bowels of MVP Arena.

"Go win a championship," Pitino told Hurley. "You've got the team to do it."

Two days later, UConn found itself in a first-half dogfight with Saint Mary's, a West Coast Conference team led by center Mitchell Saxen and a sweet-shooting freshman guard named Aidan Mahaney. A tightly contested first half ended with Mahaney knocking down a 3-pointer, only to be immediately answered by a 3 from Tristen Newton that gave the Huskies a 31–30 edge.

With just under 5 minutes left in the half, however, Alex Ducas, Saint Mary's third-leading scorer and top shooter, crumpled to the floor in pain with an apparent lower back injury. Ducas, who led the Gaels with 8 points at the time, never returned.

Saint Mary's actually led early in the latter half until the Huskies used a 14–2 spurt to break away. Once again, Hawkins had been scoreless until canning a 3-pointer with 11:28 left to put UConn up 51–40. He'd later add consecutive 3s to put the Huskies up 15 with 6½ minutes left and finished with 12 points, all in the final 11 minutes of play.

Sanogo went 11-for-16 from the floor and finished with 24 points and 8 rebounds while dominating the big-man matchup with Saxen (6 points, 3 rebounds, 4 fouls).

A 70–55 victory had the Huskies heading to the Sweet 16 for the first time since 2014, the year of their last national title. This time, the destination was Las Vegas. The opponent was Arkansas, a team built in almost the exact opposite way that Hurley had built UConn.

16

What Happens in Vegas . . .

The glitz and glamour of Las Vegas isn't what college basketball teams are expected to experience when in town for the NCAA tournament. It's a business trip, after all.

Still, UConn couldn't have expected the "welcome" it got when it arrived in Sin City on March 21, 2023, in advance of its Sweet 16 showdown with Arkansas two days later.

When the Huskies arrived at their hotel, they immediately found several of their rooms to be in deplorable condition. Some of the rooms looked like a scene out of the movie *The Hangover*. No tigers, random chickens, or abandoned babies, perhaps, but dirt, vomit—and worse.

The NCAA is in charge of booking hotels for each team, and after UConn apprised it of the situation, the Huskies were moved to a nearby, high-level hotel.

"It's not something we want to make a big deal out of," athletic director David Benedict said. "Everything worked out fine."

Still, it became international news. And things got worse.

That same day, while practicing at the University of Nevada–Las Vegas, the team bus was vandalized and some personal items were stolen, including a laptop and an iPad.

That famous "Welcome to Las Vegas" sign on the Strip suddenly didn't seem so . . . welcoming.

Hurley didn't let it become a distraction, and the focus quickly shifted to Arkansas. Like UConn, the Razorbacks had an emotional coach. Eric Musselman ripped the shirt off his back while celebrating Arkansas' upset win over top-seeded Kansas the prior weekend. And it wasn't the first time he'd done so.

"My wife's not always happy about that," Musselman conceded.

Hurley had never ripped his shirt off after a win, but obviously, his emotions were well known.

That's where the coaches were similar. The way they built their respective programs? Very different.

Before bolting for Arkansas in 2019, Musselman had had success at Nevada, largely by bringing in veteran transfers as opposed to young, high school recruits.

"I promise I wouldn't be sitting here if it wasn't for the transfer portal," Musselman said the day before his date with UConn.

At Arkansas, Musselman continued to mine the portal, including team leading scorer Ricky Council IV, injured star Trevon Brazile, and twins Makhi and Makhel Mitchell. He hadn't totally eschewed high school recruits, however, bringing in the No. 2–rated recruiting class in the country.

Contrarily, Hurley would just as soon see the portal closed forever and recruit high school talent to grow and develop. His incoming, 2023 recruiting class was rated No. 4 in the country by 247Sports.com.

But Hurley wasn't about to completely ignore the portal and the chance to bring in veteran players who could augment the homegrown talent. The 2022–2023 roster included four transfers: Tristen Newton, Hassan Diarra, Nahiem Alleyne, and Joey California himself, Joey Calcaterra.

Still, the prior season, UConn was one of the few "Power 6" programs *not* to bring in a single player through the portal. Hurley takes a lot of pride in roster construction and player retention. Only a small handful of Husky players have transferred out of the program over Hurley's first seven seasons. Javonte Brown left in midseason in 2020–2021 for Texas A&M; by the 2024–2025 season, he was working on his fourth different team (Rhode Island) in five years. Corey Floyd Jr. surprised the staff by leaving for rival Providence after redshirting as a freshman.

A few others have left, with Hurley and the staff's blessing, looking for more playing time, including Josh Carlton (Houston), Rahsool Diggins (Massachusetts), and Jalen Gaffney (Florida Atlantic). With NIL money even bigger by the end of the 2024–2025 season, the Huskies would see several players hit the transfer portal—again, all with Hurley's blessing.

But by and large, players stay at UConn, even if they don't see much playing time as a freshman or sophomore. The culture is strong enough—and the success rate in developing players proven enough—to compel them to stick it out.

However the respective rosters were constructed, it appeared UConn-Arkansas could be a real barnburner. Until it wasn't.

Unlike UConn's first two NCAA tourney games, this one wasn't close at halftime. The Huskies used an early 14-point run to take a 46–29 lead into the break and kept their foot on the gas, never trailing and upping their lead to as much as 29 before settling for a convincing 88–65 victory.

Ho-hum, another 20-plus point win. Surely, fifth-seeded Gonzaga would provide a stiffer challenge two days later.

Coach Mark Few had built a powerhouse at the Spokane, Washington–based school over the prior quarter century, taking the Zags to a remarkable 24 straight NCAA tournament appearances. All that was missing was a national title.

The Zags had been to the national championship game twice over the prior six seasons but lost to North Carolina in 2017 and Baylor in 2021.

Despite being separated by some 3,000 miles, Gonzaga and UConn actually had a fairly intriguing history. The Huskies had ended the Zags' first real run (just before Few's arrival) with a 67–62 Sweet 16 victory in 1999, en route to UConn's first title. The teams met in four other preseason tournaments over the years and, in fact, had signed on for a "home-and-home" series over the next two seasons, in Seattle in December 2023 and at Madison Square Garden a year later.

Gonzaga was led by veteran Drew Timme, the 6-foot-11 forward who seemed to have been in college hoops forever. The Zags had beaten UCLA in the Sweet 16 on a buzzer-beater by Julian Strawther, and they now set their sights on avenging that Sweet 16 loss to UConn 24 years earlier.

No chance.

UConn led by seven at halftime, then pulled away with a blitz that ballooned the Huskies' lead to as much as 23 early in the second half and culminated with an 82–54 victory.

Jordan Hawkins's 20 points led the Huskies' well-balanced scoring attack, which saw eight different players score at least 6 points.

In his final game as a collegian, Timme was hampered by foul trouble, picking up three in the first half, then his fourth early in the second to render him largely ineffective (12 points on 5-for-14 shooting).

UConn's week in Vegas began with filthy hotel rooms and stolen laptops. It ended with a pair of convincing, blowout victories.

Now, the Huskies were heading for Houston, to the same building where they had won the program's third national title a dozen years earlier.

For the sixth time in program history, UConn was going to the Final Four.

17

Avenging George Mason

The UConn men's basketball team's history since its "Dream Season" of 1990 is filled with classic games and landmark victories: conference and early-season tournaments, Big East wars, and, of course, Final Fours and national championships.

There are far fewer ignominious losses in the Huskies' history. Likely the worst came on March 26, 2006, when top-seeded UConn, brimming with future NBA talent, got popped in overtime by upstart, 11th-seeded George Mason in an Elite Eight battle at the Verizon Center in Washington, DC.

UConn featured Rudy Gay, Josh Boone, Hilton Armstrong, and Marcus Williams, all of whom would be selected in the first round of the NBA Draft a few months later, not to mention Denham Brown, a second-round pick.

George Mason had no such stars, no frontcourt players taller than 6 feet 7. But it was the Patriots, perhaps in part because UConn had too many players with their minds already in the NBA, who would advance to the Final Four in Indianapolis.

The coach of that George Mason team was Jim Larranaga, the same Jim Larranaga who now coached Miami, UConn's upcoming opponent in a national semifinal bout at Houston's NRG Stadium.

Once again, Larranaga was the underdog heading into this bout with UConn. Not nearly to the degree of 2006, of course. Miami finished tied for first in the Atlantic Coast Conference regular season, sported a 25–6 overall record, and earned a fifth seed in the Midwest Region. The Hurricanes had knocked off the region's top two seeds, Houston and Texas, to earn its date in the Final Four.

Still, Larranaga was embracing the underdog role once again. Miami's slogan for the tournament: "Don't pick us."

Miami was led by a talented group of guards. The leader in that room was Isaiah Wong, the team's top scorer (16.3 points per game) and the ACC's Player of the Year. And he was a very familiar face to UConn's coaching staff.

UConn recruited Wong hard four years earlier, hoping to bring the 6-foot-4 guard in with its 2019 recruiting class alongside James Bouknight. The Huskies were still in the American Athletic Conference at the time.

"We tried hard," Hurley recalled. "He was one of those early guys that we really wanted badly. I don't know, maybe if we were in the Big East we would have gotten him. It hurt, though, because he was a No. 1 guard target."

The Huskies wanted to bring in two guards in that class. Ultimately, they got Bouknight, a future NBA lottery pick, and Jalen Gaffney, who, ironically, was also in Houston that week with upstart Florida Atlantic. Gaffney had transferred after three middling seasons with the Huskies.

Wong had eschewed UConn's advances.

"I felt like Miami was the best decision for me," he said at the Final Four. "When I made that decision, it was pretty close."

Can't get 'em all.

Now, the goal was to stop Wong and Jordan Miller and Nijel Pack and Wooga Poplar, Miami's quartet of talented guards. Meanwhile, UConn's top guard was in danger of not playing at all.

Jordan Hawkins, the Huskies' second-leading scorer and a soon-to-be NBA lottery pick, suffered from food poisoning after a steak and calamari dinner at an upscale, Houston-area steakhouse earlier in the week. Hawkins blamed the calamari and vowed he'd never eat it again.

He missed UConn's practice and media availability on Friday, but got through shootaround on Saturday afternoon and, despite feeling "like death the past two days," per Hurley, was in the Huskies' starting lineup that night.

Before an NRG Stadium crowd of 73,860 in the nightcap of the Final Four doubleheader, UConn jumped out to a 9–0 start as Hawkins knocked down the first 3-pointer he tried, then Adama Sanogo (of all people) buried consecutive treys.

"No matter what [assistant coaches] Kimani Young and Luke Murray tell you," Hurley would say after the game, "it was not their idea to have Adama make two 3s to start the game. In a stadium."

Sanogo's 13 points led the way as UConn built a 37–24 halftime lead after one of Alex Karaban's patented, buzzer-beating 3-pointers. With so many blowout victories on the season, UConn didn't have many chances for game-winning shots. But Karaban showed a knack for knocking down numerous shots as either the shot clock or the game clock was winding down.

UConn quickly pumped its lead to 46–26 early in the latter half, but Miami wasn't quite done. The Hurricanes stiffened their defensive pressure, pulled off an 11–3 run, and closed to as little as eight (53–45) after a Wong 3-pointer with 11:38 left.

Miami would get no closer. The Huskies' 72–59 victory sent them to the program's fifth national championship game, all in the past 24 years.

Sanogo led UConn with 21 points and 10 rebounds. Hawkins battled his way to 13 points, despite looking winded at times throughout the game.

"We could tell by the way he was moving in shootaround that he wasn't going to miss this game," Karaban reported. "That's big-time confidence for us, to have one of our leaders step up, not feeling well. It's something special."

UConn's championship game opponent two nights later would be San Diego State, the No. 5 seed out of the South Region. Lamont Butler's buzzer-beater had given the Aztecs a come-from-behind, 72–71 victory over Jalen Gaffney and Florida Atlantic in Saturday's early game.

Now, only San Diego State stood in front of UConn's fifth national championship.

"The real win we want," Tristen Newton said after beating Miami, "is on Monday."

18
"We've Got Our Own!"

Dan Hurley has long been a student not only of college basketball history but also of UConn basketball history, long before he took over the reins as head coach. Heck, he was an eyewitness to two of the seminal moments.

In the crowd at Meadowlands Arena on March 22, 1990, in East Rutherford, New Jersey, to watch his brother, Bobby, lead Duke in the East Regionals, Hurley was seated behind the basket where Scott Burrell made his famous, full-court pass to Tate George, who turned around and hit a 17-footer at the buzzer to give UConn a Sweet 16 win over Clemson.

Two nights later, Duke's Christian Laettner gave UConn a taste of its own medicine, hitting an elbow jumper at the buzzer to thwart the Huskies' bid for their first Final Four and end their "Dream Season" in nightmarish fashion.

"I had a great look at the Laettner shot . . . unfortunately," Hurley recalled.

Every day Hurley has entered the Werth Family Champions Center or Gampel Pavilion as UConn's head coach, he's reminded of the program's incredible history. Trophies, championship memorabilia, and video montages of past Husky greats fill Werth's front foyer. Championship banners and retired numbers adorn the walls of Gampel.

"You walk around the building and it's a museum," he said. "It's a museum of what other people accomplished. Incredible people."

Hurley always treated the Huskies' history with great respect. He frequently refers to Jim Calhoun as "The GOAT (Greatest of All Time)," and has even praised Kevin Ollie for his 2014 title, despite Ollie's ugly ending with the program.

But Hurley yearned to create his own slice of UConn history. On April 3, 2023, inside Houston's NRG Stadium, he had his chance. And there didn't seem any way in the world that San Diego State was going to stand in his way.

The Aztecs didn't, although they wound up giving UConn its toughest time in the NCAA tourney.

San Diego State trailed by 16 points with 3:18 left in the first half after an ugly skein of offensive play, but they scored the final four points heading into halftime.

The Aztecs would get to within as little as five (60–55) with 5:19 to play. But Hawkins, who had been struggling much of the game, knocked down a huge 3-pointer off a screen that kicked off a 9–0 run and pretty much sealed UConn's 76–59 victory and fifth national title.

Tristen Newton finished with 19 points and 10 rebounds (and five turnovers, to keep things interesting), while Adama Sanogo added 17 points and 10 boards and was named the Final Four's Most Outstanding Player.

"He's obviously cemented himself into the pantheon of the greatest big guys, with all the production and back-to-back first-team all-league, and now this," Hurley said of the 6-foot-9 junior center. "To have the national championship just puts him in a position in one of the most storied programs in college basketball. He's an all-time great."

Newton and Hawkins (16 points) joined Sanogo on the All-Tournament team.

UConn had just completed one of the most dominant runs in NCAA tournament history. The Huskies became the first team ever to win all six NCAA tourney games by 13 points or more, finishing with an average victory margin of exactly 20 points per game, fourth best since the tournament field expanded to 64 teams in 1985. They trailed for exactly 22 minutes total in their six NCAA tourney games, falling behind Saint Mary's for exactly 38 seconds in the second half of their Round-of-32 bout and never again trailing in the second half of any of their tournament games.

Shortly after the confetti had fallen from the rafters, and just before the customary "One Shining Moment" blared from the stadium's speakers, Hurley got up on the championship podium at center court.

"We've been striving for No. 5!" he shouted. "Now, we've got our own!"

Later, at one end of the celebratory postgame locker room, Alex Karaban, also a student of college hoops history, was asked where these Huskies might rank in that history.

"We've got to be considered one of the most dominant teams from this March Madness run," he said. "I can walk into Gampel 50 years from now and show my kids, 'Look, I helped win this banner for us.' It's just unreal."

While Sanogo, Hawkins, and, ultimately, Andre Jackson Jr. would leave for the NBA, Joey Calcaterra would graduate, and Nahiem Alleyne would transfer (!) to St. John's (!!), Karaban, Newton, Diarra, and Clingan would be returning, leading Karaban to wonder if the Huskies could accomplish something the UConn women's team did several years earlier.

"Maybe we can pull off some Breanna Stewart, 4-for-4 [national titles]," he posited. "That's gonna be damn near impossible, but you've got to dream big in this program."

On the other side of the locker room sat Clingan, the 7-foot-2 life of the party, sporting shades, a backwards baseball cap, and an oversized, GLD chain around his neck. He was reminded of his plea to Hurley and the staff back on July 1, 2021, when he announced his commitment to UConn at Hurley's backyard barbecue: "Let's go get No. 5."

"But," Clingan confessed, "I did not think it would be my freshman year."

Barely a year earlier, he was celebrating Bristol Central's state championship at Mohegan Sun Arena. Now, he was celebrating a collegiate national title inside the 73,000-seat NRG Stadium.

In the moments after the final buzzer had sounded, Clingan had rushed into the stands to tell his father, Bill, and other family members how much he loved them.

Of course, one special family member was missing. Or was she? Clingan was sure that his late mother, Stacey, was watching from above.

"She's proud," said Donovan. "She's smiling down on me."

Outside the locker room, reporters asked Hurley about the program's history during a large, impromptu media gathering.

"Not a lot of it is ours," he noted. "We've got [James Bouknight] up as a lottery pick. Looks like Jordan may be joining him up there. Now, we've got the hardware. Now, we're gonna hang a banner in that practice gym. When I look out that window [of my office] every day, I'm gonna see a banner that we put up in there."

"Now," Dan Hurley continued, "we start to build our own trophy case."

Joey California

The UConn men's basketball program has had plenty of success with transfers since Dan Hurley took over the program in 2018.

R. J. Cole and Tyrese Martin were key figures in getting the Huskies back on the map with consecutive NCAA tournament appearances in 2021 and 2022. Tristen Newton, Hassan Diarra, and Nahiem Alleyne helped the Huskies to the 2023 national championship; Newton, Diarra, and Cam Spencer were huge factors in the 2024 title.

Newton and Spencer were probably the two most productive transfers of the Hurley tenure. But perhaps the most popular was Joey Calcaterra.

Or, as Hurley tabbed him early in his one season in Storrs: "Joey California."

Calcaterra, a native of Novato, California, about 20 minutes outside of San Francisco, had played four seasons at the University of San Diego. In the spring of 2022, he was about to sign with Vanderbilt for his grad transfer season when Hurley swooped in at the last minute and got him to take an official visit. Calcaterra only had to watch one practice to realize he wanted to be a Husky.

It didn't take long for Calcaterra to become a popular figure with his coaches and teammates, as well as UConn fans. His cocky swagger on the court and California cool off it quickly earned him one of the best nicknames in UConn basketball history.

"He really does have a huge impact on everybody he comes in contact with," Calcaterra's father, Rich, told CT Insider. "'Joey California' has really been something special, for him and his family. He's embraced it, in a fun way."

"Joey California" T-shirts and other gear helped Calcaterra earn a lucrative NIL payday. And it extended beyond Connecticut's borders. Friends and neighbors out in California took to calling Joey's parents Richie and Wendy California. In a January 11, 2023, game in Milwaukee against Marquette, Wendy, a Milwaukee product, was in the house with about 20 family and friends, all sporting "Joey California" gear.

At the 2023 Final Four in Houston, legendary actor/comedian Bill Murray was seen wearing a "Joey California" T-shirt.

Of course, a great nickname falls a little flat if the player doesn't produce on the floor. Calcaterra produced. He was a key cog in UConn's wins out in Portland, Oregon. He saved UConn's bacon on December 20, 2022, against Georgetown in Storrs, scoring 14 points in 17 minutes off the bench to help the Huskies avoid an embarrassing home upset.

As the season progressed, Calcaterra's minutes began to fade a bit (he didn't even see the floor in a February 18 win over Seton Hall). But by March, he was a key sharpshooter off the bench once again, shooting 50 percent (9-for-18) from three-point range over the Huskies' six NCAA Tournament wins.

After shooting 35.7 percent from long distance over his four seasons at San Diego, Calcaterra shot a whopping 44.6 percent from three-point land for the Huskies in 2022–2023.

And that was it. Calcaterra had exhausted his college eligibility after his one season in Storrs. The following season another grad transfer, Spencer, would come in and have even more of an impact on the floor, averaging 14.3 points per game, shooting 44 percent from distance and earning first-team All–Big East honors. Spencer parlayed all that into a second-round draft selection by the Memphis Grizzlies.

But few players had more of a one-season impact—on the floor, off the floor, and with the fans—than Joey California.

And none ever had a better nickname.

19

Art of Recruiting

With such an emphasis on bringing in high school talent and developing them, while sprinkling in a few transfers to fill the gaps, Dan Hurley puts huge emphasis on recruiting. And UConn, even before the national championship, had turned it into an art form.

Once Hurley and his staff got a recruit on campus for an official visit, they rarely didn't seal it with a commitment in the end. Andre Jackson Jr., an upstate New Yorker, admitted he was torn between Syracuse and UConn when he and his mother, Tricia Altieri, drove to Storrs for an official visit in October 2019.

"After the visit," Altieri told *CT Insider*, "on his way home in the car service, he said, 'I'm going to UConn. One hundred percent, I'm going to UConn.'"

Many UConn players had similar stories.

"I feel like a lot of times, we're behind a little bit going into an official visit," Hurley noted. "If there's four schools, we may be No. 2 or 3 coming in."

But if the staff really wants a recruit, they're often able to end up No. 1 on that recruit's list.

By the fall of 2021, with the program clearly on the rise, Hurley started fishing for recruits in deeper waters, expanding the Huskies' wish list beyond just the Northeast to a more national level. One of their prime targets was Stephon Castle, a 6-foot-6 guard from Georgia who was a national top-10 recruit in the 2023 class.

UConn got Castle and his parents, Stacey and Quannette, on campus for an official visit in November 2021. But that wasn't everyone.

Stacey Castle and UConn associate head coach Kimani Young, who had been AAU teammates some 30 years earlier in New York City, concocted a plan to bring in a surprise guest: Ann James, Stephon's grandmother, Quannette's mom. James lived in New York City and hadn't seen Stephon since before the COVID-19 pandemic shut things down some 20 months earlier. Stacey was in New York for his goddaughter's baby shower just before the visit and brought James to Storrs afterward to surprise both Stephon and Quannette.

When Stephon returned to his hotel during the visit one afternoon, his grandmother was waiting for him in the lobby.

"It was crazy," Stephon reported. "I was shocked and happy to see her."

It also served as a birthday surprise for Stephon, who had turned 17 a week earlier.

"To me, it's the small things; it's all about relationships," Quannette Castle told *CT Insider* right after the visit. "I just felt like that was very thoughtful for them to think 'Hey, it's his birthday. [They] live so far away and [they're] right here in Connecticut. Let's go ahead and try to bring his grandma there.' It makes me feel like family."

Castle had made official visits to other schools, like Georgia and Auburn, much closer to his Atlanta home.

"All the schools definitely do nice things," Quannette said, "but I thought, by far, this was one of the most thoughtful things that any school has done for him."

Indeed, while Castle waited a couple of weeks to officially announce it, he had decided to commit to UConn that weekend.

Castle, who wound up a McDonald's All-American in 2023, was the first (and biggest) recruit in what would become a bumper recruiting class for UConn. In the summer of 2022, the Huskies got pledges from Solo Ball and Jayden Ross, teammates for two years at St. James School in Maryland and for one summer on the Team Melo AAU squad. Ball, a 6-foot-4, lefty long-range shooter with supreme athleticism, was a national top-50 recruit. Ross, a long, bouncy, 6-foot-7 wing with boundless energy and enthusiasm, was a bit more of a project.

UConn had its eyes on a couple more prospects: Youssouf Singare, a raw, 6-foot-10 rim-runner from New York via Adama Sanogo's native country of Mali, and, of more interest, Jaylin Stewart, a versatile, 6-foot-7 forward from Seattle.

The staff really liked Stewart and was able to get him on campus the weekend of September 10, 2022. And that turned out to be perhaps UConn's pièce de resistance in terms of recruiting visits.

In an impressive display of foresight, mixed with some undeniable scheduling luck, UConn invited the four other 2023 recruits to visit the same weekend as Stewart. Castle flew up from Georgia. Ball and Ross drove in from their respective prep schools in New Hampshire and New York. Singare, who had yet to commit, also drove in for an unofficial visit.

The recruits, some of whom barely knew each other, bonded at UConn practices and at a UConn football game. In between all that, assistant coach Luke Murray orchestrated a photo shoot of the five players, a common practice on recruiting visits. When the group entered Gampel Pavilion for the photo shoot, they saw an array of photos of Michigan's famed "Fab Five" recruiting class from the early 1990s—Chis Webber, Jalen Rose, Juwan Howard, Jimmy King, and Ray Jackson.

The group posed for photos mimicking those "Fab Five" photos from some 30 years earlier. In the most recognizable photo, Stewart sat sprawled out in the front, ball in hand, imitating Rose's pose. Seated behind him, playing the role of Webber, was Singare. Ball stood next to him, à la Jackson, and Ross next to him, à la King.

And on the far left was Castle, seated just as Howard was in that famous photo.

"That was Coach Murray's idea, and it just came to life," Ball reported. "We've got to have our own confidence that we're just as good as the previous Fab Five."

The following day, those "Fab Five" photos went viral on social media, eliciting joy on UConn Twitter and some consternation from others (including Hurley) who weren't crazy about the "Fab Five" label so soon.

"We tried to solidify and get them to commit by getting a brotherhood together," Ball said. "We really had a good time over the football weekend. Although the game wasn't good, we all had a good time . . . to the point that I thought they weren't going to go anywhere else."

Indeed, a week later, Stewart committed to UConn. A week after that, Singare did the same.

UConn's own "Fab Five," the No. 3–rated recruiting class in the country, per 247Sports.com, was complete. The program's recruiting prowess had continued, though Hurley was quick to point out that it wasn't all about gimmicks, surprises, and viral photos.

"What wins for us," Hurley noted, "is when they get a chance to spend time with our full staff and players, a chance to watch practice, go to dinner with the staff, feel the vibe, feel the culture. It's something people want to be a part of."

The Fab Five watched approvingly from afar as UConn marched to its dominant, 2023 national title run.

And on the heels of that run, Dan Hurley's recruiting eyes got even bigger. He was ready to home in on his biggest target yet.

The No. 1 recruit in all the land.

20

One Big Loss

In the glow of the 2023 national title, UConn was a program clicking on all cylinders. At the NBA Draft in June 2023, Jordan Hawkins became the program's 15th all-time lottery pick (and second under Hurley, along with James Bouknight) when he was selected 14th overall by the New Orleans Pelicans.

Andre Jackson Jr., despite his shooting deficiencies, was taken in the second round by the Orlando Magic and quickly traded to the Milwaukee Bucks, where he'd emerge as a key role player.

Adama Sanogo, despite being named the Final Four's Most Outstanding Player and a two-time first-team All–Big East selection, went undrafted. But he quickly signed with the Chicago Bulls on a two-way contract and, two years later, became the all-time leading rebounder for the Windy City Bulls, Chicago's G-League affiliate.

Hurley had proven he could not only win a national title but also develop players into NBA talent. Jackson had only been a top-50 recruit, while Sanogo somehow didn't even crack the top 100. Before that, Tyrese Martin, a three-star recruit when he committed to Hurley at Rhode Island, had developed into a 2022 second-round draft pick after two seasons with Hurley at UConn.

With all that in mind, Hurley started fishing in deeper waters. The deepest of all.

He decided to take a shot at Cooper Flagg, the top-rated recruit in the Class of 2024, a potentially generational talent who was already predicted to be the No. 1 overall pick in the 2025 draft—despite not even turning 18 until December 2024.

Flagg was a 6-foot-8 shooter from Maine now starring for the No. 1 prep program in the country, Montverde Academy in Florida. He boasted dynamic athleticism and a killer instinct, and what set him apart even more was his defensive ability as a long-armed rim-protector.

Only problem was, virtually everyone in the country was convinced he was going to Duke. Including, it seemed, Flagg, who had stated in previous interviews that Duke was his "dream school."

But when Flagg announced that he'd be making official visits in the fall of 2023 to UConn (September 22–24), Kansas (October 6–8), and Duke (October 20–22), the Huskies at least had a shot.

And when Flagg later canceled that scheduled visit to Kansas, it was down to a good ol' UConn-Duke battle.

And UConn had more than a puncher's chance, in part due to a kinship between Flagg's family and the family of Donovan Clingan.

Flagg's mother, Kelly Bowman, had played college basketball alongside Clingan's late mother, Stacey Porrini, at the University of Maine some 25 years earlier. Their coach was Joanne P. McCallie—who later coached at Duke.

Clingan's parents, Bill and Stacey, had attended Kelly and Ralph Flagg's wedding. When Cooper Flagg arrived at Gampel Pavilion on September 22, he was greeted by Clingan, as chronicled by social media video.

As numerous other visitors had done in previous years, Flagg went to the UConn football team's game the next day at Rentschler Field. The Huskies' opponent? Couldn't make this up: Duke.

Predictably, the lowly UConn gridders got stomped by the Blue Devils, 41-7. At one point during the game, the somewhat sparse student section broke out in a chant of "Coo-per Flagg! Coo-per Flagg!"

But none of that was going to have any bearing on Flagg's decision. His family had stated they wanted Flagg to be in a winning program that continued his development (for what almost certainly would be the one-and-done year he was on campus).

Flagg left Storrs on September 24 without having made a decision. His assistant coach at Montverde, Kevin Boyle Jr., told *CT Insider* that Flagg told him his visit was "positive" but didn't reveal much else.

Rumors and off-the-record sources insisted that Flagg loved UConn and was legitimately torn. His dad, Ralph, "liked" his son's post on Twitter that read: "The personal connection ('the guy who can best develop me') to the (head coach) is going to be the slim differentiator."

Duke was no longer coached by legendary Mike Krzyzewski but, rather, by former player Jon Scheyer.

Cooper Flagg's October 20 visit to Duke coincided with the program's annual "Countdown to Craziness," the Blue Devils' version of "Midnight Madness" at Cameron Indoor Stadium. Flagg, the 16-year-old wunderkind, was the star attraction.

More than a week passed and still no official word. On October 30, Hurley made his visit to the Middlesex County Chamber of Commerce member breakfast at the Sheraton Hartford South hotel in Rocky Hill, Connecticut. It's an annual event just prior to the start of the college basketball season, where Hurley typically gives a quick breakdown of each player on the roster, then answers a few questions from the crowd of about 300 enjoying a buffet breakfast.

That format held form on this morning, but one of the first questions from the audience took Hurley a bit by surprise.

"When are we going to know about Cooper?" a local businessman stood up and asked.

Hurley was speechless for a moment, before ultimately smiling and replying, "You probably know more than I do."

What the attendee, and perhaps Hurley, didn't know at the time was that, just a few minutes earlier, Flagg had announced his decision via social media.

He was going to Duke. Unlike the 1999 national championship game or the 2004 Final Four, the Huskies had lost to the Blue Devils.

Barely. Later that day, Ralph Flagg posted on Twitter: "I don't think people will truly ever understand how close it was."

Duke won not only the recruiting battle but, a year later, the Atlantic Coast Conference regular season (19–1) and conference championships behind Flagg, who was the consensus National Freshman of the Year as well as the Associated Press National *Player* of the Year, leading Duke in scoring (19.1 points per game), rebounding, assists, and even blocks as an 18-year-old freshman.

Flagg also led the Blue Devils to the Final Four, where they ultimately squandered a late, 14-point lead and fell to Houston, 70–67.

Did UConn really lose in the situation? Of course, Hurley very much wanted Flagg, and there was no way for him to admit otherwise. But the Huskies had never really gotten this far with a nation's top recruit. Typically, those players were pickings for the likes of Duke, Kentucky, North Carolina, and Kansas. Now, the Huskies were going head-to-head with those programs. They finished second this time, but Hurley wasn't necessarily conceding defeat in the big picture.

"UConn is second to no other program in college basketball," he said that day. "We don't decide who we get, but no one should be off the board, relative to whether they should be considering us. We do it, right now, as good as anybody."

During Jim Calhoun's heyday, straight through to Hurley, the Huskies had typically relied on top 30–75 recruits, along with a couple of top-100/150-type longer-term projects, to yield success. And it certainly had worked, to the tune of five national titles.

"Obviously, we have to stick to our identity and what's worked for us," Hurley continued. "The range we've recruited in has paid dividends. There may be incredible value in the 52nd-ranked player in the country. To you, he may be a guy who's a two-year player and you love his ability, and maybe in another class, the players in that range, you may not like and say I'm going to shoot higher, and if I don't win there, I'm going in the portal, because I don't think that these high school players can help us."

Then, he took a bit of a swipe at Duke and, in particular, star guard Jared McCain, who had emerged as a star on TikTok.

"We're blue-collar basketball, not social-media basketball."

Dan Hurley wasn't about to take a defeat, even a rare recruiting defeat, sitting down.

21
Repeat after Me

Cooper Flagg wouldn't be coming to UConn, but the "Fab Five" had arrived in Storrs in the summer of 2023. Stephon Castle was seen as a probable starter right off the bat. Solo Ball, Jayden Ross, and Jaylin Stewart were also in line for minutes as freshmen. It took Stewart a little longer to get in the flow, however; he arrived on campus a bit later after Seattle's school schedule was extended due to a teacher's strike and then suffered a minor injury upon his arrival to campus.

Donovan Clingan had announced his return at the championship parade back in April, excited to take over the starting center role after backing up Adama Sanogo for all 39 games as a freshman. Tristen Newton took a little longer to decide, taking a stab at the NBA Draft combine, but he ultimately decided to run it back as well. Samson Johnson, the 6-foot-10 rim-runner who missed much of UConn's championship run due to injury, was back and ready to serve as Clingan's backup.

Alex Karaban, who started all but the very first game of his freshman year, was back, as was Hassan Diarra. The team had plenty of talent overall, much of it young, but some of it with national championship pedigree.

But the Huskies had lost a lot of talent as well. Jordan Hawkins, Andre Jackson Jr., and Adama Sanogo were all in the NBA. Nahiem Alleyne had transferred to St. John's, looking for more minutes under

Hall of Fame coach Rick Pitino. And Joey "California" was in . . . well, California.

Joey Calcaterra's college eligibility was exhausted, and now he was on the South Bay Lakers, the Los Angeles Lakers' G-League affiliate. With Calcaterra, Hawkins, and Alleyne gone, the Huskies needed to bring in some shooters. It appeared they had found one in Nick Timberlake, a Massachusetts product who had shot 41.6 percent from the three-point line the prior season at Towson and had been granted a sixth and final year of college eligibility.

Timberlake seemed ticketed to UConn through the transfer portal—until he wasn't. Kansas stepped in at the last minute and swooped the 6-foot-4 guard away.

It was perhaps the best loss UConn and Hurley has ever had.

The Huskies immediately shifted their focus to Cam Spencer, a 6-foot-4 guard who had led the Patriot League in scoring two years earlier at Loyola (Maryland), then transferred to Rutgers and shot 43.4 percent from the three-point line. He visited UConn in June and quickly committed, intent on winning a national title of his own.

By the end of the season, Spencer had just about managed to make UConn fans forget that Joey California (and Nick Timberlake, for that matter) ever existed.

And so, these were the guys who Dan Hurley had assembled to try to repeat as national champions: returnees Tristen Newton, Donovan Clingan, Alex Karaban, Hassan Diarra, and Samson Johnson; graduate transfer Cam Spencer; and freshmen Stephon Castle, Solo Ball, Jaylin Stewart, Jayden Ross, and Youssouf Singare.

Pretty impressive, but a lot of production gone. The Huskies went on a summer bonding trip to Europe, where they won every game (albeit against subpar competition). They were ranked No. 6 in the preseason AP Top 25 poll. Kansas, with its new addition, Nick Timberlake, was No. 1. Defending Big East regular-season and conference champion Marquette was one spot above the Huskies at No. 5.

In the Big East preseason coaches' poll, however, UConn was picked to finish third, behind Marquette and Creighton. Marquette had garnered 96 points and seven first-place votes, Creighton 92 points and four first-place votes. UConn earned 79 points but zero first-place votes. Villanova, on the heels of a first-round NIT ouster, was picked fourth with 76 points.

The defending national champion Huskies were predicted to finish closer to fourth place than second place in their own league, something Dan Hurley would repeat numerous times in the ensuing months and years.

Hurley had been gifted a sign of disrespect to add to the ever-present chip on his shoulder. Still, it was going to be an extremely difficult task to repeat as national champs.

Only six men's basketball programs had won back-to-back national titles: Oklahoma State (1945–1946), Kentucky (1948–1949), San Francisco (1955–1956), Cincinnati (1961–1962), UCLA (1964–1965, 1967–1973), Duke (1991–1992), and Florida (2006–2007). The only two living coaches who had accomplished the feat, Duke's Mike Krzyzewski and Florida's Billy Donovan, spoke to *CT Insider* about how tough it would be for Hurley & Co.

"That second year for us was a really, really, really hard year. Beyond hard," Donovan noted. "I don't think those guys could have ever understood how hard it was going to be."

His biggest challenge?

"Can we move past the previous year, or are we going to be brought back into the past?" Donovan recalled wondering. "It's always going to be, 'Florida, national champions.' Danny's going to go through this. Before UConn's name is ever mentioned, it's going to say, 'Defending national champion, UConn Huskies.' You can get brought back in there, and sometimes people feel like the confetti's still falling."

Donovan, who would be elected to the Naismith Basketball Hall of Fame in April 2025, had an advantage right off the bat, bringing back most of his 2006 title team the following season, even without the lure of "name, image, and likeness" (NIL) money. Joakim Noah, Al Horford, and Taurean Green, all future NBA players, all returned.

Krzyzewski also had a host of star returnees, including future Hall of Famer Grant Hill and Christian Laettner, arguably one of the greatest college players of all time. And, of course, he had Bobby Hurley, Dan's older brother and an all-time great college point guard.

It was a different world back then, before NIL and the transfer portal wreaked havoc on roster retention.

"Even if it's not a different world," Krzyzewski warned, "it's very difficult."

Krzyzewski, also a Hall of Famer, is the winningest men's basketball coach (1,202) of all time (UConn's Geno Auriemma is tops among both women's and men's coaches), and only John Wooden (10) has more men's national titles than Coach K's five. Still, he knew how difficult it was to repeat.

"Look, it's a one-game, six-game thing," Krzyzewski said. "Anything can happen in a game—an injury, a call, the other team is just a little bit better than you. So, to win the whole thing is crazy. And, if you do it twice in a row, that's nuts. He's lost some of his guys. The thing is, you rack 'em up and start playing again. He's going to be at Connecticut for a long time, so they'll have really outstanding teams over and over."

Donovan has been close with Hurley since recruiting some of Hurley's players at St. Benedict's Prep. He served as somewhat of a sounding board when Hurley was deciding whether to remain at Rhode Island or come to UConn.

He would also offer Hurley advice as the ensuing season went on, clearly believing Hurley was capable of pulling off what he and Krzyzewski had done.

"If Danny gets back to the Final Four again, I'll bet you he'll be much, much more prepared for Saturday–Monday than he was this year," Donovan predicted. "He'll know exactly what they're walking into."

22

In the Phog

UConn's pursuit of a second straight national title officially began on November 6, 2023, with a 95–52 romp over Northern Arizona at Gampel. Unofficially, the pursuit had started some six months earlier, when UConn's players convened on campus for summer classes and sessions and remained there throughout almost the entire summer and fall, along with that European trip.

"It's an 11-month season here," Hurley frequently says.

Through it all, there was the parade through downtown Hartford, ceremonial first pitches at Fenway Park and Yankee Stadium, the ringing of the New York Stock Exchange bell, and a visit to the White House, where President Joe Biden became the fourth different commander in chief to congratulate a UConn men's team as national champs.

Dan Hurley, a creature of habit if there ever was one, stuck to his tried-and-true scheduling strategy: five or six games against high-major and/or "power conference" teams; five or six "buy games" (paying a team to come play you at your home arena) against some of the lowest of the low-majors in the country; then, of course, the grueling, 20-game Big East schedule.

It's a strategy used by a lot of high-major coaches as a way to boost their team's all-important NCAA Evaluation Tool (NET) ranking, one of the chief tools used by the NCAA Tournament Selection Committee to determine eligibility and seeding for the 68-team field. The NET favors blowout wins, so teams like UConn try to feast on those five or six weak sisters early on.

Sure enough, the Huskies dominated their first three opponents by an average of 39 points per game. Things would presumably get tougher at the Saatva Empire Classic at Madison Square Garden, however, where UConn would face Indiana in its first game.

And the Huskies would have to do so without Stephon Castle, who scored 29 points combined in his first two games as UConn's starting point guard. Castle injured his knee in the waning minutes of the Huskies' 107–67 blowout of Stonehill and would be out at least the next couple of weeks.

Solo Ball, another freshman, entered the starting lineup in Castle's place and, for the most part, made the most of it, scoring 9 points in UConn's 77–57 romp over Indiana. Tristen Newton was the real star, however. The 6-foot-5 guard notched a double-double with 23 points and 11 rebounds, not to mention 6 assists.

The following night, the Huskies faced 15th-ranked Texas for the tournament title. Behind 20 points from Alex Karaban and a career-high 15 points and 8 rebounds from Samson Johnson off the bench, UConn snared a "close" 81–71 victory. Close in that it kept alive (barely) the Huskies' remarkable streak of 22 straight double-digit, non-conference victories, dating back to that 2022 NCAA tourney loss to New Mexico State.

It was also yet another multi-team event (MTE) victory for the Huskies, driving their record up to 13–3 in such events since Hurley took over.

UConn would push that double-digit, non-conference win streak to 24 with easy wins over Manhattan and New Hampshire. But its biggest test loomed: a Big East/Big 12 Battle at historic Phog Allen Fieldhouse in Lawrence, Kansas, on December 1, 2023, against fifth-ranked Kansas.

This would be a meeting between the two prior national champions. Kansas had won it all in 2022, its second national title under Hall of Fame coach Bill Self. It would also feature a 7-foot-2 battle between UConn's Donovan Clingan and Kansas junior Hunter Dickinson, who had transferred from Michigan the prior spring.

It was easy to see why Kansas was 149–6 against non-conference opponents at "The Phog" since Self took over the program 21 years earlier. A sellout crowd of 16,300 jammed the historic building and was loud and active all night, from the pregame introductions to the final buzzer. The famous "Rock! Hawk! Jayhawk! K-U!" chant reverberated around the arena, but that was just one of several ritualistic chants the crowd exercised throughout the night. Ted Lasso himself (actor Jason Sudeikis) was in the house to rile the fans up even more.

Meanwhile, UConn was still without Castle, who had hoped to return for the game but was not quite ready. And making matters worse, Cam Spencer, the Huskies' leading scorer, entered the game with a minor foot issue, then aggravated his other foot early in the game and hobbled around the floor for the rest of the way.

The Huskies seemed a bit razzed by the home crowd in the early goings.

"It really knocked us on our heels," Hurley would later admit. "We don't go to many places this organized, with fan involvement. I think it rattled us for a while."

UConn trailed by 12 late in the first half but had cut it to just seven (38–31) by halftime.

Then, Tristen Newton took over.

The graduate guard almost single-handedly brought the Huskies back, scoring eight straight UConn points in one stretch that gave his team its first lead. The Huskies would up their lead to five (52–47) with about 8½ minutes left.

But Kansas soon countered with an 11–0 run to give it a six-point advantage with just over a minute left. UConn wasn't done. The Jayhawks missed three of four free throws inside the final 30 seconds, Newton scored on a fast-break layup, and, somehow, the Huskies had a chance for a game-winning shot in the final seconds.

Spencer would do the honors, despite suffering a rough shooting night through obvious pain. The 6-foot-4 grad transfer had an open look for a 3-pointer with 2 seconds left.

It was off the mark, by quite a bit. Kansas owned a 69–65 victory.

So this is what it took to snap UConn's 13-game winning streak dating back to the previous season, along with its 24-game double-digit, non-conference win streak: a four-point loss to the fifth-ranked team in the nation, in front of arguably the loudest, most intimidating crowd in the sport, with its future lottery-pick guard sidelined by injury and its leading scorer hobbled by a foot issue.

And still, a chance to win the game with 2 seconds left.

"We were fortunate," Self admitted. "They got a shot off. That's the last thing you would want is for Spencer to get a look."

It was a noble effort by the Huskies to rally back and nearly win. But Hurley wasn't about "nearly" winning.

"Just like Kansas, at UConn we don't do the moral victories or silver linings," Hurley said. "I thought our guys showed a champion's heart by putting ourselves in position to have a 3 to steal it and get out of here with a win. I liked the champion's heart. I wish we would have played better. I do believe that last year's team on December 1 was better than this year's team on December 1. But, I do think this year's team has a chance to be as good as last year's team, when we're fully healthy and playing in March."

Self seemed to agree.

"I would think that he thought his team got better by being here tonight," he said of Hurley, "even though he's probably not happy with the outcome."

Newton announced himself to the world with 31 points, hitting six of nine 3-pointers. Dickinson won the battle of giants with 15 points and 9 rebounds to Clingan's 8 and 7, respectively.

Spencer finished just 2-for-12 from the floor, 1-for-7 from the three-point line, and even missed his first two free throws of the season.

Nick Timberlake? Two scoreless minutes.

23

Saving Christmas

Four nights later, December 5, 2023, the Huskies were back at Madison Square Garden to face their second straight blue blood program. This time it was North Carolina, ranked ninth in the nation and led by big man Armando Bacot and guard R. J. Davis, in the annual Jimmy V Classic.

Stephon Castle made his return after missing the prior six games, but he was limited to just 10 minutes off the bench. UConn was fine without his contributions, thanks in no small part to the fellow freshman who had temporarily taken over Castle's starting spot.

Solo Ball had had mixed results over the prior six games, with nice games against Indiana and Texas, followed by some struggles, most notably at Kansas, where the atmosphere may have been a bit too much for him.

Ball would start three more games after this one, often struggling with his shot, the game speeding up on him a bit, before Castle returned to the starting five. But against Carolina, under the bright lights of the World's Most Famous Arena, Ball didn't lie.

The lefty shooter knocked down a trio of 3-pointers and finished with a career-best 13 points as UConn rolled to an 87–76 victory.

Ball was hardly the star of the show. Spencer bounced back quickly from his foot woes with 23 points, 7 rebounds, and 6 assists. The fiery guard continued to endear himself even more to the UConn fan base, at one point screaming in Bacot's face during a small kerfuffle that would live forever in Meme Land.

Alex Karaban added 18 points and Tristen Newton 14. Another victory at the Garden.

After a 38-point thumping of Arkansas Pine-Bluff, the Huskies flew out to the West Coast to face No. 10 Gonzaga in the Seattle Tip-Off on December 15, 2023. This was a homecoming for Jaylin Stewart, the freshman who left home 3,000 miles away to play at UConn. Stewart hadn't played much in the early going of the season and, as Hurley would later admittedly regret, didn't play much against Gonzaga at Climate Pledge Arena.

But the Huskies had little trouble handling the Zags for the second time in eight months. This one wasn't quite as dominating as the 28-point, Elite Eight mauling the prior March in Vegas, but UConn never trailed in a 76–63 victory this time around.

Donovan Clingan, the 7-foot-2 sophomore, loomed as large as the famous Space Needle, finishing with a game-high 21 points and 8 rebounds and holding Gonzaga standout center Graham Ike to a near-invisible five points. Clingan's alley-oop dunk off a lob from Hassan Diarra inside the final 4 minutes gave the Huskies a 12-point lead, and they were never again threatened.

UConn had finished non-conference play 10–1. It had defeated three top-20 teams, two of them (North Carolina and Gonzaga) ranked in the top 10. The Huskies were a Cam Spencer missed jumper away from a perfect 11–0 mark.

Now, it was on to the Big East. The first two games were against the teams that had handed the Huskies perhaps their two most painful losses in that dreadful January a year earlier: Seton Hall and St. John's.

Dan Hurley, of course, had missed the prior year's game against Seton Hall at Newark, New Jersey's Prudential Center, watching at home with COVID while the Huskies somehow lost a game in which they trailed for a mere 7 seconds.

He was on the sidelines for this December 20, 2023, Big East opener in Newark against his alma mater, which was coached by Shaheen

Holloway, who had succeeded Hurley as Seton Hall's point guard some 25 years earlier.

The Huskies jumped out to a 20–10 start but trailed by five at halftime as noted Husky-killer Kadary Richmond went to work. Donovan Clingan dominated the paint to start the second half, scoring UConn's first 6 points. But about 3½ minutes into the half, that production (along with Clingan's 7-foot-2 frame) came tumbling to the floor.

Clingan was called for a foul and fell to the ground, grabbing his right ankle and wincing in pain. He tried to get up but couldn't, ultimately limping back to the locker room with trainer James Doran.

Clingan returned to the bench about midway through the half and tried to convince Hurley to put him back in the game, to no avail.

Seton Hall took advantage of the big man's absence and handed UConn its worst loss since a January 4, 2020, defeat at South Florida—by the exact same score, 75–60.

"We've all got to own it," a disconsolate Hurley said in the postgame press conference, while facing many familiar faces from the New Jersey/New York media. "That was not reminiscent of a top team. That was a pretty embarrassing performance for all of us, myself first in line. To have one of my teams in a conference opener go on the road and perform like this, I'm having a hard time even looking (the media) in the eyes when you ask me a question. There's a real feeling of shame there."

Richmond, who had scored 17 points in a row and a career-high 27 against UConn two years earlier, finished with 23 points and a whopping 8 steals.

Worse, Clingan would later be diagnosed with a tendon injury in his right foot, sidelining him for the next three to four weeks, including a pre-Christmas bout three days later in Hartford against St. John's and its new coach, Rick Pitino.

Pitino had taken over the St. John's job not long after being vanquished by UConn with Iona in the opening round of the 2023 NCAA tourney. He brought with him Taliek Brown, the former UConn standout guard who had been on Hurley's staff for three seasons before joining Pitino's staff for a season at Iona, then following the Hall of Famer to St. John's.

There was another familiar face on the Red Storm roster. Nahiem Alleyne, a key guard off the bench during UConn's 2023 title run who sought more playing time and was one of several transfers to Pitino.

"We wouldn't have won a championship without him," Hurley said of Alleyne.

With Clingan out, Samson Johnson got just his second collegiate start (and first of the season) and immediately kicked off the festivities with a powerful putback dunk.

Stephon Castle made his return to the starting lineup and knocked down a bunch of key baskets down the stretch.

In between, UConn struggled offensively and certainly missed Clingan's presence on the other end of the floor. St. John's led by six at halftime, but the Huskies kicked off the latter half on a 10–2 run to notch one of seven lead changes over the final 20 minutes.

When Glenn Taylor Jr. hit a 3-pointer with 4:13 left, the Red Storm led 63–61. It would be their final lead.

Castle had an acrobatic tip-in of a Newton missed 3-pointer to tie the game, and Newton put the Huskies ahead for good with a driving layup as UConn pulled out a 69–65 victory.

Staring down the barrel of an 0–2 start in Big East play, Hurley was relieved in the postgame press conference.

"We saved Christmas for ourselves, and for our great fans and for the state of Connecticut," he said. "Because a loss here would have been a lot of doom and gloom for a lot of people."

UConn didn't necessarily ruin Pitino's holiday, the veteran coach insisted.

"I'm going to have a really good Christmas, because of the improvement with the basketball team," Pitino told reporters, before jetting down to his Miami home for the holidays.

It wouldn't be the last time UConn faced Pitino this season. Ultimately, the Huskies would ruin more than just Christmas for the Hall of Fame coach.

24

Back at No. 1

The win over St. John's kicked off a remarkable run for the fourth-ranked Huskies. They won their next 12 games, in a variety of ways: at home, on the road (Butler, Xavier, Villanova, St. John's, Georgetown, DePaul), by blowout, and, occasionally, by narrow victory.

Alex Karaban's late-game heroics led to an 88–81 win at Butler on January 5, 2024, his mom Olga's birthday.

"I called her this morning and said, 'I'll get a win,'" Karaban reported after the game. "That's all she wanted."

On January 14, the Huskies scored an 80–67 win in Hartford over Georgetown. That victory, coupled with losses to unranked opponents by the three teams ahead of them in the AP poll (Purdue, Kansas, and Houston) meant UConn was due for some great news the following afternoon.

Sure enough, on January 15, UConn took over as the No. 1 team in the nation for the first time in nearly 15 years. It was the 10th time UConn had been ranked No. 1 in the land, and the first since March 8, 2009. The first time had come on February 13, 1995.

UConn received 39 of the 63 first-place votes. Purdue dropped to No. 2, with 20 first-place votes. It began to look more and more like these two programs were on a collision course for March. Or April.

Dan Hurley insisted the No. 1 ranking didn't mean much to him, noting that only the "squirrels" obsess over such things (whatever that meant). But there's little doubt it meant a lot to him, especially after stating his case why the Huskies should be the top-ranked team following the win over Georgetown.

Two nights later, UConn began defending its No. 1 ranking against No. 18 Creighton at Gampel. Clingan made his return in this one, despite practicing just a couple of times over the prior month. UConn had gone 5–0 without the 7-foot-2 sophomore, but Clingan quickly made everyone remember what they had missed.

Coming off the bench, Clingan finished with 6 points, 5 rebounds, and 2 blocks in 16 minutes. But his mere presence had a great effect on the game, particularly defensively. UConn held Creighton to 36 percent shooting and forced 14 turnovers. In one 12½-minute stretch, spanning the end of the first half and beginning of the second, UConn outscored the Bluejays 18–4.

The Huskies outrebounded Creighton 47–22, including a whopping 21 off the offensive glass. Old pal Ryan Kalkbrenner was limited to just five shots and a quiet 11 points.

"We weren't very good," Creighton coach Greg McDermott rued. "UConn had almost everything to do with that."

On January 20, one of the wildest, most remarkable days in the long history of the Big East unfolded. A pair of noon games separated by a mere 15 miles, Marquette–St. John's at Madison Square Garden and Creighton–Seton Hall at the Prudential Center in Newark, ended in wild fashion. Marquette survived three straight missed free throws down the stretch by 93 percent foul shooter Tyler Kolek and escaped with a 73–72 win over St. John's—but only after Daniss Jenkins's 3-pointer at the buzzer was off the mark.

Creighton bounced back from its ugly loss at UConn to win a triple-overtime thriller over the Pirates, who actually entered the game in first place by virtue of their pre-Christmas win over UConn.

That night at Wells Fargo Center in Philadelphia, UConn pulled out a 66–65 win over Villanova that wasn't quite that close, with 'Nova guard Mark Armstrong's unnecessary 3-pointer at the buzzer providing the final score.

It put the cap on an incredible 24 hours for the league. Throw in Xavier's 92–91 win over Georgetown the night before and that was four different games separated by a total of six points, three of them by one point, one of them going to three overtimes.

"C'mon, man, this league right here . . . there's nothing like this league," Hurley said after the Huskies had taken over sole possession of first place. "Everyone bows their chest out about their league, but show me a more compelling league. Show me a league where the games are played at this level of ferocity and intensity. The coaches are so good, the environments are incredible."

Some might argue the Big 12, which had won two of the prior three national championships (Kansas in 2022, Baylor in 2021) and had put a team in three straight national finals (Texas Tech lost to Virginia in 2019; there was no NCAA tournament in 2020).

Hurley scoffed at that suggestion.

"Don't ask me questions about the Big 12," he said. "Touchy subject."

Indeed, UConn had been seriously considered for the Big 12 that prior summer. League commissioner Brett Yormack, a New Jersey product and former CEO of the New Jersey/Brooklyn Nets, seemed willing to overlook UConn's atrocious recent football history and realized college basketball still had tremendous value.

Ultimately, the Big 12 opted for a trio of Pac-12 teams (Utah, Arizona, and Arizona State, the latter coached by Dan Hurley's older brother, Bobby) instead. Once again, UConn had been abandoned at the altar, just like it had been in 2012 when the ACC chose Louisville over the Huskies, or in 2016 when the Big 12 first looked to expand but wound up taking nobody.

But while Hurley said all the right things and understood how moving to a power conference would provide much-needed financial security for the entire athletics program, he seemed happy where his feet were.

"It's the best conference," Hurley said of the Big East. "It's the hardest games. There's nothing to compare these games to. These types of games are ones that are going to make all of us really dangerous in March."

"These are not like SEC or ACC-type of games, either," he continued. "This is a manhood test every time you step on the court in the Big East. It's UFC-type [stuff]. Like, steel cage. You can throw elbows, it's jujitsu, muay thai, it's everything. It's tough, especially on the road."

A couple of weeks later, after a week's break, then wins over Xavier (by 44 points!) and Providence, UConn traveled to Madison Square Garden for a road game against a team that was starting to emerge as a true rival once again.

Not long after UConn's "Christmas-saving" win over St. John's in Hartford, Pitino told the New York media that the Red Storm's home game with the Huskies next season wouldn't be held at MSG, per usual, but rather at the 5,600-seat, on-campus Carnesecca Arena.

"I have my reasons," Pitino told reporters.

The primary reason seemed to be Pitino's fear of UConn fans overwhelming St. John's fans at MSG. At Carnesecca, St. John's could control ticket sales better while also providing a more charged-up atmosphere with students ostensibly making the smaller arena louder and more intimidating.

Asked about Pitino's vow, Hurley said, "The last thing I'm thinking about is where I'm playing somebody next year."

But he quickly added that everyone was "gunning" for UConn, which had won five national championships since 1999, and that St. John's hadn't had much success in that time. Indeed, the Red Storm hadn't even won an NCAA tourney game since 2000.

"We've had unbelievable success here in basketball," Hurley noted. "There are programs who haven't been to a Final Four or haven't been to the NCAA tournament in 20 years, so there's obviously a lot of punching up."

Shots fired.

25

Rick Rolled

UConn's 74–65 win over Providence on January 31, 2024, closed the Huskies out at 8–0 in January, a far cry from their January of discontent a year earlier.

Now, on to St. John's.

Pitino had revealed his reason for wanting to play UConn at Carnesecca Arena was to celebrate Lou Carnesecca's 100th birthday in January 2025, while noting that UConn "couldn't take a compliment." But he later conceded that the Johnnies' game with UConn would, indeed, be at Madison Square Garden next season.

That didn't keep him from throwing a few jabs Hurley's way.

In what appeared to be a barb aimed at Hurley, Pitino had told reporters a couple of weeks earlier that coaches who constantly argue with referees are "cheating."

Asked about Pitino's comments the day before facing St. John's at MSG, Hurley replied: "We all have egos. I don't think any of us are in this to become friends. I've got a level of respect for anyone that coaches at this level."

According to Taliek Brown, the former UConn standout player and Hurley staff member who was now an assistant at St. John's, Pitino's quotes over the prior month were all calculated.

"He's just hyping it up," Brown told *CT Insider*. "He's just a competitor, that's what it is. We know UConn is No. 1. He's just competing."

Such was the groundwork for a Sunday, February 3 UConn–St. John's battle at the World's Most Famous Arena. The Huskies would be without Alex Karaban ("the brain center of the program . . . the ultimate problem-solver," per Hurley) who had injured his ankle in the Providence win.

Others had to step up, and they did. Most notably, Stephon Castle.

For the second straight game, the true freshman notched a career-best scoring effort, this time with 21 points. Castle, a 6-foot-6 guard, was also forced to guard St. John's 6-foot-11 center and leading scorer Joel Soriano late in the game, with Donovan Clingan and Samson Johnson both saddled with foul trouble.

Soriano didn't score a single point with Castle guarding him.

Castle was starting to round into the form of an NBA lottery pick that many expected upon his arrival at UConn but had gotten sidetracked a bit by his early-season injury. His effort helped lead UConn to a 77–64 win before 19,812 fans (many of them bedecked in UConn blue, to Pitino's dismay).

Afterward, Hurley was again asked about Pitino's recent salty comments toward him and his program.

"It's a fascinating league," Hurley replied. "Some of the stuff we do pisses each other off. Recruiting, sometimes, you don't like how someone recruited a player. Same thing in-game, they may not like how I coach with the refs, with the emotion. It causes friction. I think it's good. It brought a lot of interest into this game, it packed the arena, and I'm sure a lot of people watched."

Hurley was asked if he thought it was ironic that Pitino, known for sideline antics of his own in his younger days, has now been criticizing Hurley's behavior.

"I watched him," Hurley said. "I tried to emulate some things that he's done in his career, just like you study all the great coaches. Whatever, man. I don't think we're going to become best friends this summer."

"But," Hurley added, "I respect the hell out of him."

Rick Rolled

The Huskies would push their winning streak to 14 games. Things were going so well that, during a February 10 game at lowly Georgetown, Hurley practically had to fabricate adversity. With about 6 minutes left in the game, incensed at what he perceived as lack of hustle, he called time-out and reamed his players in the huddle.

"Foot stays on gas!" he screamed. "Foot stays on gas!"

The Huskies led by 25 points at the time and wound up with an 89–64 victory.

On February 19, for the first time in program history, they were the unanimous No. 1 team in the nation.

That would be short-lived.

UConn's February 20 trip to Omaha, Nebraska, to face Creighton was miserable, as usual. In fact, this one might have been the Huskies' worst visit of all to CHI Health Center, where they had never won.

UConn scored the game's first seven points and Creighton missed its first three 3-pointers. After that, not much went right for UConn, or wrong for the 15th-ranked Bluejays.

Creighton hit its next six 3-point attempts and wound up hitting a whopping 14 treys for the game. The Bluejays rolled to an 85–66 victory that few could have seen coming, at least in such emphatic fashion.

"Losing is never a good feeling," shrugged Tristen Newton, who finished with 27 points and 12 rebounds, "but [we're not] invincible."

Creighton fans stormed the court after the victory, which surprised Hurley.

"I guess that means you're pretty good," he surmised.

He was even more surprised at the reception he had received from the rowdy, sellout crowd all night. A "F— Dan Hurley!" chant started during the national anthem and continued throughout the game. So much for Midwest Nice.

When the game was over, Hurley got in a shouting match with fans. While leaving the court to the locker room area, he shouted at a few rowdy fans while pointing to a burly security guard escorting him out: "If you come over [the railing], he'll knock you out!"

The video went viral. A few days later, Hurley said that while entering and leaving the CHI Health Center court, he felt like Cersei

Lannister, the fictitious character from HBO's *Game of Thrones*, going through the "walk of shame."

"Minus the spitting. I don't think anyone spit," quipped Hurley, who later posted a meme on social media showing Cersei walking through an angry mob, only with Hurley's face Photoshopped over hers.

Hurley suggested, however, that Creighton or the Big East should have some sort of canopy built over the walkway from the court to the locker room.

"Once you get to the arena floor, if folks want to serenade me with 'F— Dan Hurley' chants, if the university and the people there think that that's classy, then go for it. If during the anthem, fans want to honor the anthem there by several times screaming 'F [Hurley],' that's the institution, the arena, the security. But, I think the league, to avoid me in a confrontational situation, should probably look at the to-and-from part."

Indeed, when UConn returned to CHI Health Center the following season, a canopy had been put up over the area.

Anyway, the 19-point loss was the biggest loss by a No. 1 team since Virginia lost to 16th-seeded University of Maryland, Baltimore County (UMBC) in a first-round tournament game in 2018. Of course, Virginia would bounce back for a national title the following season.

UConn wouldn't lose again for more than nine months.

The Huskies fell two spots to No. 3 the following week. On February 24, in a blowout win over Villanova, Tristen Newton recorded his fourth career triple-double, topping his own record.

UConn was No. 2 in the land heading into a March 6 bout at eighth-ranked Marquette. Alex Karaban broke out of a shooting slump for 23 points, and Cam Spencer added 17 in a 74–67 victory.

Amazingly, somehow, it was UConn's first road win over a nationally ranked team in more than 10 years, since the Kevin Ollie–coached Huskies notched a January 14, 2014, win at Memphis en route to their own national title. UConn had dropped 22 such games since.

"I don't give a [bleep]," Hurley insisted. "It's stupid. We sucked for years; we went through some cold winters. And then when I took over this job, there was no portal, so you had to rebuild something slowly."

Spencer, whose fiery temper had made him a UConn fan favorite and opposing fan target, picked up a technical after screaming at Marquette fans and its bench following his 3-pointer that put UConn up 14. Hurley, no stranger to technicals himself, wasn't happy.

"He's got to rein that in," the coach said. "There are some other fan bases and programs that I don't mind him [bleep]-talking them. But I didn't like him doing it near their bench, to their fans. Because these people here . . . it's a classy program, it's a championship program."

Spencer concurred.

"Bad timing on my part, for sure," he confessed. "I apologized to the guys. My emotions got the best of me. It won't happen again."

It didn't. At least not in college. The NBA would be a different story, where Spencer, a 2024 second-round draft pick by Memphis, got into verbal sparring bouts the following year with several players, including future Hall of Famer Kevin Durant.

When UConn rolled over Seton Hall by 30 on Senior Day on March 3, the Huskies had completed their stated goal of finishing the season unbeaten (16–0) at home. A win at Providence a week later (which featured Hurley barking at another fan toward the end of the Huskies' 14-point victory) put the finishing touches on another one of their goals: a Big East regular-season championship.

UConn's 18–2 record was its best ever in league play. In fact, the Huskies became the first Big East team ever to win 18 league games in a season. Not Patrick Ewing's Georgetown teams. Not Chris Mullin's St. John's teams. Not even Ray Allen or Emeka Okafor's UConn teams.

Just Dan Hurley's 2023–2024 UConn team. And even loftier goals remained.

26

Another Jewel in the Crown

UConn racked up the hardware at the Big East awards presentation on March 13, 2024, at Madison Square Garden. Hassan Diarra won the league's Sixth Man Award. Stephon Castle, in perhaps the easiest vote ever, was named Freshman of the Year. Hurley got his due as Big East Coach of the Year.

But per usual, the Huskies felt snubbed in one major category. Tristen Newton, the leading scorer on the first 18-win team in league history, didn't win Player of the Year. That went to Devin Carter, the league's leading scorer and soon-to-be NBA lottery pick whose Providence team finished 10–10 in the Big East standings and ultimately wasn't selected for the NCAA tournament.

No problem, Newton insisted. Much bigger honors and awards were headed his way.

UConn walloped poor, injury-plagued Xavier once again in its Big East tourney opener the next day, 87–60. That set up another meeting with good ol' Rick Pitino, this time on Friday night in the Big East semifinals at Madison Square Garden—as great an atmosphere as there is in college sports.

And this one didn't disappoint.

No-look passes, alley-oop dunks, technical fouls on both coaches and the curious case of the Man in the Red Blazer ensued over 40 fun-filled minutes.

Ultimately, UConn prevailed with an utterly entertaining, if draining, 95–90 victory.

Newton, perhaps inspired by his Player of the Year snub, finished with 25 points, 9 assists, and 6 rebounds. Cam Spencer, who Rick Pitino had called his favorite player in the Big East the day before, added 20 points and 9 assists.

But the highlight (lowlight?) of the game came midway through the first half, when Pitino loudly objected to a foul call. He was quickly hit with a technical foul.

"I haven't had a technical in a really long time; I was really looking forward to that moment," Pitino said afterward, adding that he "wanted to get" the technical with his team not getting a favorable whistle.

While Pitino argued his case with the officials, Dan Hurley's best ally, seated courtside, started gesturing and yelling toward the coach.

"And then I had to go against Bobby Hurley," Pitino said, referring to Dan's father. "He brings in another Hall of Famer going against me."

While all this was going on, as if not wanting to be left out of the fun, Dan Hurley was called for a technical of his own, upset about a fan in the front row.

"There was a short guy in a red blazer that was yelling at the refs," Hurley later explained. "And then he started yelling at me and moving in my direction. So, I was just pointing out to James [Breeding, an official] that he was behaving worse than Coach Pitino."

The fan was Dan O'Grady, a longtime friend of Pitino who insisted he didn't instigate Hurley.

"I did not say a word to Dan. Not a word," O'Grady told the *New York Post*. "I said to the referee, 'He's out of the box,' and he gave him a T. That was it. If someone was cursing at him, it wasn't me."

Hurley called for O'Grady's ejection and seemed to get his way as the fan appeared to be escorted away—until O'Grady returned to his courtside seat, about 15 feet from the St. John's bench, at the start of the latter half.

Hurley had rescinded his ejection request and told the ushers to let him remain.

"I wanted him to stay, not because I thought he was a good guy," the ever-superstitious Hurley noted. "I thought it might be bad luck. Karma."

Things normalized in the second half as the Huskies turned a five-point halftime lead into 10 late in the game, then hung on for victory. The 90 points St. John's scored were the most by any UConn opponent since Auburn's 109 points in that double-overtime, UConn victory in the Bahamas on Thanksgiving Day 2021.

But perhaps the most incredible statistic was this: starting with that March 17, 2023, win over Pitino's Iona in a first-round NCAA tourney game in Albany, and capped by this March 15, 2024, win over St. John's, Hurley and the Huskies had beaten Pitino four times in the span of a year.

No other program had ever accomplished that feat against the Hall of Famer.

If Hurley took any satisfaction out of that, considering Pitino's barbs throughout the season, he didn't let on. He was focused on notching the next "jewel" in the Huskies' crown: a Big East tournament championship, something that had evaded Hurley since he took over six years earlier.

The prior season, he had been denied both the league regular-season and tournament championships by Marquette. Now, he had a chance to avenge the previous year's Big East semifinal loss to the Golden Eagles in the championship game. It was UConn's first trip to the Big East tourney finals since 2011, when Kemba Walker led an unprecedented, five-wins-in-five-nights run to a title.

Compared to the emotion and drama of Friday night's semifinal win over St. John's, this one was anticlimactic.

Marquette was without Big East Player of the Year Tyler Kolek, the nation's leader in assists who was sidelined by an oblique strain. Both teams were sluggish at the start, combining to miss 13 of the game's first 14 shots. After the first media time-out, just over 5 minutes into the game, the score was a whopping 2–0.

But Tristen Newton's 3-pointer at the buzzer gave UConn a 26–24 halftime lead, and the Huskies shot a blistering 63 percent (17-for-27) in the latter half to run away with a 73–57 victory.

"They caused a lot of pain to us last year when they beat us," Alex Karaban said of the Golden Eagles. "It always stuck with us throughout the summer and during the March Madness run. But, to get that monkey off our back and be able to beat them, it felt good."

Tristen Newton, *not* the Big East's Player of the Year, was named the Big East Tournament's Most Outstanding Player. After scoring 8 points against St. John's, freshman Jaylin Stewart continued to solidify his spot as the eighth man in UConn's rotation with 9 points against Marquette, hitting three of four 3-pointers.

Donovan Clingan had notched a double-double by halftime and finished with 22 points and 16 rebounds. He became the first player with at least 20 points and 15 rebounds in a Big East championship game since Georgetown's Patrick Ewing in 1984.

"To have my name (alongside) someone who's a legend in basketball, college basketball and the next level, means a lot," Clingan said.

The Huskies matched Georgetown in another area: their eighth Big East tournament crown matched the Hoyas for most in league history.

Said Hurley: "Just to be part of the history and tradition of some of the coaches and players that have won championships in this league is an awesome feeling."

27

No Sleep 'til Brooklyn

UConn finished 7–0 in Madison Square Garden for the season. But its work in New York City wasn't done.

Practically from the time the final piece of confetti had fallen to the floor at Houston's NRG Stadium the previous April, Hurley had preached the mantra: "Brooklyn to Boston to Phoenix." That meant if UConn took care of business in 2023–2024, it would be the top seed in the East Region and play its first two rounds at Brooklyn's Barclays Center, the regional semifinals and finals at Boston's TD Garden, and the Final Four at Phoenix's State Farm Stadium (actually in Glendale, Arizona).

And the next evening, on Selection Sunday, that's exactly the path that the NCAA Selection Committee laid out for the Huskies.

UConn was the No. 1 overall seed for the NCAA tournament. And the Huskies wouldn't have St. John's (or hardly any Big East teams) to push around anymore this time around.

St. John's, Seton Hall, and Providence all sat watching the NCAA Tournament Selection Show on Sunday, March 17, 2024, with reasonable expectations of hearing their names called. None of them did.

The conference wound up with just three bids: No. 1 overall seed UConn; Marquette, a two-seed; and Creighton, a three-seed. That's it.

A league that had once sent 11 teams to the NCAA tournament in 2011 and had routinely sent five or six teams each year over the past couple of decades was limited to a mere three bids.

"I think you're probably just a little embarrassed for such a proud league," said Dan Hurley, who had said the night before that the league deserved six bids. "The whole thing is kind of a shell game. It really comes down to what the committee values."

On this, Hurley and Rick Pitino agreed.

"The problem is, in speaking with people on the Selection Committee, that they had no consensus way of evaluating," Pitino told *CT Insider*. "It's almost like 12 independent contractors. They all had their own formula, and that's the problem. The committee needs to get direction, and the coaches and the programs need to know, 'OK, what's the criteria? And how is it measured?'"

A year earlier, Cam Spencer had found himself in a similar situation. In his one and only season at Rutgers, he and the Scarlet Knights watched the Selection Show expecting to hear their name called.

"We thought we were in, I won't lie," Spencer recalled. "We were really surprised when we weren't."

So surprised was Spencer that he refused to watch the tournament. Which, of course, UConn ultimately won.

Now, he was the second-leading scorer, top 3-point shooter and first-team All–Big East selection on the No. 1 overall seed in the tournament that was looking to repeat as national champs. The first step would be at Brooklyn's Barclays Center against Stetson, a school better known for churning out baseball players like Jacob deGrom than for its men's basketball program.

UConn's opening-round win was as easy as expected, with the Huskies holding a whopping 52–19 lead at halftime. Those 52 points matched the total Stetson would finish with in a 91–52 UConn victory that saw 10 different Huskies score.

Next up: Northwestern, a Big 10 team coached by Chris Collins, son of former NBA star and coach Doug Collins. Hurley, the son of a Hall of Fame high school coach, said he related to Chris Collins better than just about any coach in the country.

"It feels like you're kind of looking in a mirror," Hurley said.

Their respective teams didn't bear much resemblance in their Round-of-32 bout on March 24 at Barclays. With Donovan Clingan dominating inside and Stephon Castle shutting down Northwestern's all-time leading scorer, Boo Buie, UConn led 40–18 at halftime and pumped its lead up to 30 in the second half before settling for a 75–58 romp.

Clingan finished with 14 points, 14 rebounds, and a career-high 8 blocks. Tristen Newton also notched a double-double with 20 points and 10 assists.

Castle, just a freshman, helped hold Buie, a fifth-year senior averaging 19.4 points per game, to just 9 points on atrocious 2-for-15 shooting.

UConn shot just 3-for-22 from the three-point line, but it hardly mattered. What did matter, and not necessarily in a positive way, was that one of those 3-pointers was hit by Andre Johnson Jr.

Johnson, a second-year walk-on who grew up not far from Clingan in Bristol, Connecticut, entered the game with 43 seconds left and the Huskies up 16. Rather than dribble out the clock, as Hurley typically wanted him to do, he hurled up a long 3-pointer that hit nothing but net.

It marked Johnson's first points as a Husky, and his teammates were ecstatic for him. His coach, not as much.

As soon as the shot went up, Hurley twirled around and leaned against the scorer's table, head in hands, for a good 10 seconds. He then had a word with Johnson and seemed to apologize to Collins, not wanting to show him up. Collins didn't appear to have an issue with it, and neither did Johnson's teammates.

"That's one time," Alex Karaban quipped, "that we didn't care what Coach [Hurley] thought."

Johnson's first UConn points also turned out to be his last. After the season, he transferred to Utah Valley.

Anyway, this is what qualified as "controversy" for the UConn men's basketball program. On to Boston, where the Huskies would start off against a familiar foe.

28

A Boston Curb-Stomping

There are quite a few coaches in college basketball who had presumably seen enough of Dan Hurley and his Huskies by March 2024.

Rick Pitino, of course, had gone 0–4 against Hurley over a full calendar year. Gonzaga's Mark Few had his season (and Drew Timme's lengthy playing career) ended in a blowout loss in the Elite Eight in 2023, then got popped by Hurley and the Huskies nine months later in Seattle. Kevin Willard's fears of UConn's return to the Big East had been so justified, even losing Adama Sanogo's recruitment to the Huskies at the last minute, that he had fled to coach Maryland after the 2021–2022 season.

Poor Brian Dutcher would soon be added to that list.

Dutcher had coached San Diego State to a surprise run to the national championship game the previous season. That's where the Aztecs ran into the UConn buzzsaw in Houston, falling 76–59 in the program's first visit to the title game.

Dutcher had assembled another good team in 2023–2024, leading San Diego State to a 24–10 overall record and a fifth seed in the East Regional. The Aztecs slipped by Alabama–Birmingham in their first round game, then crushed upstart Yale, which had knocked off fourth-seeded Auburn in its opener, by 28 points (eliminating the chance for an all-Connecticut, UConn-Yale East Regional semifinal bout in the process. This was fine with Hurley, who never wanted to schedule Yale in the regular season).

Now, the Aztecs were up against UConn once again. This time, they had a true force in 6-foot-9 forward Jaedon LeDee, a role player during the prior season who was now one of the nation's leading scorers at 21.9 points per game.

When LeDee hit a jumper to kick off the scoring at Boston's TD Garden, UConn trailed in a game not only for the first time in the 2024 NCAA tournament but also for the first time since early in the second half of the Big East tournament championship game nearly two weeks earlier.

And when LeDee stayed hot with 15 first-half points, and UConn hit a 4-for-22 shooting skid late in the opening half, it appeared maybe—*maybe?*—the Huskies were finally in for a challenge.

Not so much.

After Cam Spencer's 16 points carried UConn in the first half, Stephon Castle took over in the second. Then Hassan Diarra. Then Donovan Clingan, whose two dunks late in the game clinched an 82–52 UConn rout that reserved a seat for Dutcher in the "Tired-of-Seeing-UConn" club.

"Either [they're] better or we're worse," the good-natured Dutcher shrugged afterward, on the difference between this season and the prior.

Later, Dutcher would quip that the Aztecs were "7-and-UConn" over the past two NCAA tourneys: seven wins over everyone else and two losses to the Huskies.

UConn certainly had the look of not only a national champion but also an all-time great team. Who was going to stop the Huskies? Maybe Illinois?

The Illini were certainly talented, boasting the No. 2–rated offense in KenPom's ratings, averaging 84.2 points per game with an up-tempo style engineered by Terrence Shannon Jr., the nation's third-leading scorer at 23.5 points per game. Shannon had poured 29 points in 29 minutes on Iowa State in a Sweet 16 bout two nights earlier.

Illinois may have been the No. 3 seed in the East, but it boasted the résumé of a team that could have been considered for a top seed. The

A Boston Curb-Stomping

Illini entered their March 30 Elite Eight bout with the Huskies having won seven straight games, including the Big 10 championship, and 10 of their last 11, their lone loss to No. 2 overall seed Purdue.

Then, a couple of Twitter posts ruined everything for Illinois.

The night before the game, Hurley was perusing social media when he saw a few posts from Sean Harrington, a former Illini co-captain and now an analyst on ESPNU. Harrington opined that he didn't think UConn had anyone who could stop Shannon Jr. He also noted that UConn fans were "getting nervous."

Give Dan Hurley the tiniest bit of motivation, another chip on his already chip-stacked shoulder, at your own peril.

This game was tied at 23 with just under 2 minutes left in the first half. Stephon Castle, Alex Karaban, and Tristen Newton were a combined 0-for-13 from the floor. Hassan Diarra hit a 3-pointer to kick off a 5–0 Husky mini-run to give them a 28–23 lead at halftime.

Seven minutes into the second half, UConn's lead was 53–23.

The Huskies had engineered a 30–0 run. A head-spinning, 30–0 run that had to be the most dominant 8-minute, 52-second stretch of basketball in UConn's storied history.

The Huskies scored the first 25 points of the latter half and had Illini coach Brad Underwood burning one time-out after another, with no answer in sight. Donovan Clingan helped spearhead the second-half run with 9 points, to go with a rafter-shaking block of Quincy Guerrier. In fact, Illinois stubbornly kept driving to the basket, despite the 7-foot-2 presence of Clingan, even as he swatted away five shots and even swiped three steals.

"Well," Underwood began his postgame press conference, "I didn't expect that."

Clingan finished with 22 points and 10 rebounds to go with his 5 blocks and 3 steals. The Connecticut kid who grew up a Boston Celtics fan was named the East Regional's Most Outstanding Player on the Celtics' home floor.

As for Terrence Shannon Jr.? A harmless 8 points on 2-for-12 shooting, thanks to yet another defensive masterpiece by Castle. And

Sean Harrington? His "asinine" social media posts helped fuel this UConn team of "beasts and monsters," per Hurley.

"They try to motivate themselves, because they know we're better than them and they need a super-hero game for them to win," Newton said of the Illini. "We had an off night tonight, and we still won by 25."

An off night, despite a 30–0 run. That's how dominant this UConn team was. Newton, the team's leading scorer, didn't even score a basket in the Huskies' ultimate 77–52 win. Didn't matter. UConn shot just 3-for-17 from the three-point line. Didn't matter.

About the only adversity UConn had experienced in its first four NCAA tourney games came not from Boo Buie, Jaedon LeDee, or Terrence Shannon Jr., but from Larry David. Yes, the Larry David of the HBO series *Curb Your Enthusiasm* fame.

The 76-year-old actor/writer, who also co-created *Seinfeld* with Jerry Seinfeld, was in Boston for a stand-up show at the MGM Music Hall and had nabbed tickets to the UConn-Illinois game. As if straight out of one of David's zany *Curb* episodes, he sat in his front-row seat, just behind press row, with his legs hanging over the railing.

As UConn roared through its 30–0 run, David started shouting in the direction of the Husky bench.

"Shame on you, Hurley!" he yelled, according to CBSSports.com. "Take those starters out! Stop coaching! The game is over!"

Afterward, Hurley said he never heard David during the game but was a bit disappointed.

"That guy's my hero," Hurley said. "I am the Larry David of college coaching."

Not even Larry David could curb UConn's enthusiasm at this point. The Huskies were advancing to their second straight and seventh overall trip to the Final Four, for a date with history.

29

In the Mix for Six

It wouldn't be a UConn trip to the Final Four without some sort of travel snafu getting in the way.

A year earlier, it was UConn's deplorable hotel situation, necessitating a switch, followed by its team bus being vandalized. This time, the Huskies were stranded for hours when they arrived at Bradley International Airport but their chartered plane to Phoenix didn't.

UConn's plane was supposed to fly from Kansas City to Connecticut, then take off at 6 p.m. on Wednesday, April 4, 2024, to take the team to Arizona. But it never arrived, due to a mechanical issue and issues with the crew regarding the number of hours they were able to work under Federal Aviation Administration rules.

The NCAA was responsible for finding UConn a new plane but couldn't find one for hours. Finally, a smaller plane was flown in from Cincinnati and arrived around 11 p.m., but it couldn't support the team's full travel party. Plus, rainy, windy weather and an additional minor mechanical issue kept the Huskies grounded.

Finally, around 1:30 a.m., UConn took off, flying nearly five hours across the country and arriving in Phoenix at around 3 a.m. local time.

Of course, plane issues were nothing new to UConn. The Huskies' flight home following a 64–57 win over Marquette on March 6 had been canceled due to mechanical issues, and the Huskies had to spend the night in Milwaukee. Then, their rescheduled flight the following day for 12:30 p.m. also was canceled. So, UConn booked a practice at the University of Milwaukee that afternoon and flew home afterward—not from Milwaukee, however, but 90 minutes down the road from Chicago.

Anyway, UConn was back at the Final Four. And the Huskies' first opponent featured a familiar face, particularly to Hurley.

Alabama, the West Regional champion, was coached by Nate Oats, whose connection to the Hurley family runs deep. Bobby Hurley, Dan's older brother, got to know Oats while Oats was coaching Romulus High outside of Detroit and Bobby was recruiting one of his players, E. C. Matthews, to play at Buffalo. Ultimately, Bobby hired Oats as an assistant coach at Buffalo, and Oats took over the head coaching reins a few years later after Bobby left for Arizona State. Oats had great success at Buffalo, even beating Bobby in an NCAA tournament game in 2019.

Dan Hurley typically doesn't like coaching against family, or friends of the family. He certainly won't schedule Arizona State and won't even schedule nearby Rhode Island (at least for a regular-season game) because of the ties he still has to the program.

He typically wouldn't schedule Oats and Alabama, either, though he did thump the Crimson Tide the previous season at the PK Invitational. But Hurley was ready to put aside any friendship in his pursuit of a second straight title.

"This is, like, the Final Four," Hurley reasoned. "Somebody that I really care about is going to play for a national championship. Preferably, me."

Oats insisted he would have been content to be a high school coach the rest of his career, not unlike Hurley's father, Bob Sr.

"I'm just a high school guy that caught a break, that's still trying to prove I belong at this level," Oats said.

And now, that "high school guy" had a chance to prove he belonged at the highest level of men's college basketball. Against a close friend and confidant.

Either way, somebody Dan Hurley really cared about would be playing for a national championship two nights later. Preferably Dan Hurley, according to Dan Hurley.

Oats had led Alabama to its first Final Four in program history as the face of college basketball's analytics movement, preaching the "3-pointers/layups or dunks" philosophy while eschewing less-efficient or risk-worthy midrange jump shots. The theory: making easy baskets or long-range baskets worth three points is more efficient than 12- to 15-footers worth two.

But Hurley subscribes to the same philosophy, Oats was quick to point out.

"They do it a little bit differently because they have a post player in [Donovan] Clingan they can go to," Oats noted.

On April 6, 2024, at State Farm Stadium, before a crowd of 74,720 that included several former UConn greats like Ray Allen, Rip Hamilton, Emeka Okafor, and, of more recent vintage, Jordan Hawkins, the Huskies ran into a red-hot Crimson Tide team.

Alabama shot 8-for-11 from the three-point line in the first half, and its 23–18 lead midway through the half was UConn's biggest deficit in an NCAA tourney game since trailing Saint Mary's by eight early in an eventual Round-of-32 victory the prior season.

Despite that, UConn still held a 44–40 lead at halftime and quickly pumped that up to an eight-point edge on two different occasions. Alabama would tie it back up at 56; however, then came a sequence for UConn that didn't quite match its 30–0 run in the Elite Eight win over Illinois, but was just as key.

After Stephon Castle hit a pair of free throws, 'Bama's Aaron Estrada teed up a wide-open 3-pointer that would have given the Crimson Tide the lead back. It rattled in and out, and Castle countered with a runner.

Mark Sears missed a 3-pointer off a screen, and Alex Karaban scored on a putback to put the Huskies up 64–56 and cause Oats to burn a time-out.

The Crimson Tide would get no closer than six the rest of the way as UConn ultimately scored an 86–72 victory.

"That," Donovan Clingan noted, "was a very good win."

Very good in so many ways, not the least of which that it set up the national championship game that everybody wanted: No. 1 overall seed UConn versus No. 2 overall seed Purdue.

All year—heck, even the previous year—it seemed inevitable that UConn and Purdue would meet in the national title game. In 2022–2023, the Boilermakers were the No. 1 team in the nation for most of the season, keeping UConn from the top spot even after the Huskies had swept through the PK Invitational (where, ironically, Purdue was also playing, but in a different bracket). Purdue, however, became just the second No. 1 seed to lose to a No. 16 seed in the NCAA tourney, getting popped by little ol' Fairleigh Dickinson. UConn, of course, rolled to the 2023 NCAA championship.

In 2023–2024, UConn took over No. 1 from Purdue in mid-January, ultimately ceded it back to the Boilermakers after the 19-point loss at Creighton, but snared the No. 1 overall NCAA tourney seed after winning the Big East tourney while Purdue fell to Wisconsin in the Big 10 tournament semifinals.

UConn entered the championship game 37–3, Purdue 34–4. This would be a battle of behemoths, in more ways than one.

30

Eclipsed!

At some point in the middle of the 2023–2024 season, UConn assistant coach Luke Murray pulled Donovan Clingan aside and told him to watch Purdue's 7-foot-4, 300-pound monster Zach Edey play.

"We're going to play him in the national championship," Murray said to the 7-foot-2 sophomore. "You're going to guard him one-on-one, and we're going to take away their guards."

Edey, a Canadian native, had been the dominant force in men's college basketball for the past two seasons, the back-to-back Naismith Player of the Year award winner, the second of which he was presented at a ceremony on Sunday, April 7, 2024, just a few minutes before Dan Hurley was honored as Naismith Coach of the Year.

Edey led the nation in scoring (25 points per game) and was second in rebounding (12.2). He was an unstoppable force inside who also got to the foul line more than any other player in the country—by a lot.

Clingan, while seen as the better NBA prospect and projected as the higher draft pick, was just a sophomore in his first season as a starter, not even an All–Big East selection.

And for the first time as a collegian, Clingan (who had earned the nickname "Cling Kong") would be going up against a player taller than him.

"[Ryan] Kalkbrenner's probably the closest," Clingan said of Creighton's 7-foot-1 center, the day before the title game. "I saw Shaq [O'Neal] today. He made me feel real little."

Clingan had been in Edey's company only once before, passing by him at the PK Invitational but not exchanging greetings. He had kept tabs on Edey from afar, however.

Clingan had become well versed in cutting down nets, having climbed the ladder to do so five times over the past two seasons after various UConn championships. Edey was a bit newer at it, and after Purdue had punched its ticket to the Final Four the prior weekend, he eschewed the ladder and simply snipped off a piece of net from his flat feet.

"It's cool," Clingan said, "[but] you gotta go up the ladder."

Yes, UConn's pursuit of a second straight national title was the biggest story line entering the national championship game. But right below was Clingan versus Edey. Cling Kong versus Big Maple. The kid from Bristol versus the veteran from Canada.

"I'm excited," Clingan admitted. "Me and my team are ready to compete for a national championship."

No doubt, Purdue fans were excited. They outnumbered UConn fans by about a three-to-one margin at the surrounding bars and restaurants around Glendale, and inside State Farm Stadium on Monday night. Certainly, part of it was the novelty: UConn was in its second straight championship game and sixth over the prior 25 years. Purdue was in just its second title game *ever*, and the first since Rick Mount's Boilermakers lost to Lew Alcindor's dynastic UCLA team in 1969.

UConn was looking to establish a dynasty of its own.

On April 8, 2024, as a solar eclipse cast its shadow over much of the United States (nothing to do with Clingan and Edey on the same floor together, blocking out the sun), 74,423 fans (about 50,000 or so pulling for Purdue) filled State Farm Stadium to see if history could be made—or denied.

What to do with Edey? The Huskies stuck to that plan Murray had imagined back in midseason: let him do his thing and take away the Boilermakers' guards.

Edey dominated inside in the first half en route to 16 points, scoring on alley-oop dunks, hook shots, and low-post moves. It didn't help that Samson Johnson, Clingan's backup, picked up two fouls in a five-second span, forcing Clingan to play all but one minute of the first half.

But the rest of Edey's teammates were essentially locked down by UConn's long, athletic guards like Stephon Castle and Tristen Newton. Purdue, the second-best 3-point shooting team in the nation (40.2 percent) managed only two 3-point attempts in the first half, making one. UConn led 36–30 at the break.

And as the Huskies tended to do, they started pulling away in the latter half. Alex Karaban, scoreless over the first 30 minutes of play, knocked down a 3-pointer to put UConn up 54–40. He later slammed home a dunk to put the Huskies up 15, then came up with his biggest play of the night.

Newton missed a 3-pointer, but Karaban skied for the rebound and kicked it back out, ultimately leading to a 17-point Husky lead with 6 minutes left.

Johnson wound up fouling out in just 4 minutes of action. Clingan finished with four fouls. For several minutes late in the game, the 6-foot-8 Karaban had to guard the 7-foot-4 Edey. And he wound up with the bruises to show for it.

"We couldn't afford, at that point, for Donovan to foul out," Hurley said later. "We had the lead, we really didn't care if Zach scored, if it took them 15, 18 seconds to score 2s. When you have a lead of that size, the only thing that beats you is live-ball turnovers, giving up 3s, or fouling 3-point shooters."

None of the above happened.

Edey wound up with 37 points, but the Huskies were okay with that. Well, almost okay.

"We didn't necessarily want to let him get 37," Murray quipped.

But UConn held Purdue's long-range gunners to a mere 1-for-7 from the three-point line.

"For the most part, the game plan was very much to try to force [Edey's] catches out, try to not let him turn over his left shoulder and get to his right hand easily, which he did sometimes," Murray reported. "But really, take away the three-point line."

Clingan finished with 11 points, 5 rebounds, and a block, compared to Edey's 37 points, 10 boards, 2 blocks, and 10 fouls drawn.

Edey had won the battle, but Clingan won the war: 75–60. Yet another double-digit victory. Another national title.

"He's a great player," Clingan said of Edey. "I really like how he got position tonight. He elbowed me in the head about 15 times. I might need some Advil after this."

"It's worth it," he added. "National champion."

Again. Two-for-two for Clingan. And when it was his turn to snip off a piece of the net, he pulled Edey's trick and eschewed the ladder.

"The scissors weren't good, though," he noted. "It was hard to cut today."

Such were the problems of the back-to-back national champions, the first since Florida in 2006 and 2007.

Newton finished with a game-high 20 points and was named Final Four Most Outstanding Player. Three of his fellow starters—Stephon Castle, Cam Spencer, and Clingan—joined him on the All-Tournament team. Edey was the only non-Husky named to that team.

UConn finished the season 37–3, the most wins in a single season in program history. The Huskies' 68 wins over the past two seasons were the most in any two-year span in program history. They finished 4–0 against the Big 10, three of them in the NCAA tournament (Northwestern, Illinois, Purdue). They were 19–1 over the past two seasons against Power Five foes, all 19 wins by double digits. They had won their 12th straight NCAA tourney game by double digits, as well, and won their six tourney games in 2023–2024 by an average of 23.3 points.

Really, there were too many ways to describe the Huskies' dominance, both with numbers and adjectives.

"If you just take the actual quality of play: the offensive efficiency in the halfcourt and in transition, the defensive numbers, what we did rebounding the ball, the margin of victory, the assist-to-turnover numbers, the way we dominated the NCAA Tournament," Hurley marveled, "that's one of the best teams in the last 25 years of college basketball."

For the second straight year, Karaban was approached in the victorious locker room and asked if this was an all-time great team.

"I would assume so," the junior forward said. "Just by the fashion we did it, too. Dominating, double-digit wins every game for the past two years, 12–0. It's got to be. I know Florida was dominant, Duke was dominant. It's crazy, because we still talk about these teams now. It's so hard to go back-to-back, people still talk about them."

Added Hurley, "You can't even wrap your mind around it, because you know just how hard this tournament is. What a special group of people and a special coaching staff. An incredible group of players—the best group of players you could possibly do it with."

"UConn," Hurley continued, "is a special place this time of year."

Like Father, Like Son

Andrew Hurley scored exactly 12 points in his college basketball career. But he holds a "record" at UConn that will likely never be broken.

Hurley was on the floor at the end of 12 straight NCAA tournament victories, almost always dribbling out the clock of a blowout win. That includes two national championship–game wins, in 2023 and 2024.

Hurley, the youngest of Dan's two sons, was a four-year walk-on for the Huskies. His father often said Andrew could have played Division 2, possibly even low-major Division 1 ball. Instead, he decided to stick by his father for four years, two national titles, 12 points, and 12 appearances at the end of NCAA tourney games.

But those were hardly Andrew Hurley's only accomplishments as a UConn walk-on.

"He's done so much damage control for me," Dan Hurley told reporters, while fighting back tears, in March 2024. "He humanizes me a little bit with the players."

Indeed, after Dan may have chewed out his team in the locker room following a game or a practice, Andrew had to remain with his teammates once the coach left the room.

"I think being able to connect with the guys and kind of being that voice, the voice between the coach and the players, a lot of that has to do with just the players in the locker room accepting me and listening to what I have to say sometimes and accepting what I have to do," Andrew said. "I started off

doing anything I could, just practicing hard or just kind of earning some sort of respect just to be able to be a voice."

The end of UConn blowout victories throughout Andrew's tenure often featured the Husky student section chanting, "We want Hurley!," sometimes with as much as five minutes left to play. Dan would always oblige, putting his son in usually over the final one or two minutes of a blowout.

And those blowouts continued throughout the 2023 and 2024 NCAA tournaments, with UConn winning every game by double digits. Usually, Andrew and another walk-on, Andre Johnson Jr., would enter the game with about a minute or so left and pretty much run out the clock, no damage done. But in the 2024 Final Four, there was one minor "incident."

With 18 seconds left in the Huskies' 86–72 win over Alabama, Andrew entered the game along with Solo Ball, Jaylin Stewart, Jayden Ross, and Apostolos Roumoglou, prepared to dribble out the clock yet again.

Alabama star guard Mark Sears, however, got a little overaggressive trying to steal the ball from Hurley, committed a foul, and had words with the walk-on.

Afterward, Hurley took the high road.

"They were competing until the end of the horn," Andrew said. "I made a mistake letting up a little bit. They're a really good team, so I've got to be stronger with the ball."

The Huskies inbounded the ball with about a second left and Hurley caught it, but it was after the final buzzer sounded. So, does that mean he officially dribbled out the clock again?

"Maybe that counts, I don't know," he said with a smile. "I hope so."

Two nights later, there was Andrew again, dribbling out the final seconds of the win over Purdue.

"It's ridiculous," he said. "I'm so thankful for these guys, last year and this year, it's been such an unbelievable experience. It's crazy, because not everybody gets to play in this tournament, and I get thrown out there . . . it's just crazy to be a part of it."

The following season, Andrew joined his dad on the bench as a graduate manager.

31

"Me Season"

Another title, another championship parade in downtown Hartford. This one was attended by Tarris Reed Jr., a 6-foot-10 transfer from Michigan. It turned out to be a pretty impressive recruiting visit; Reed committed to UConn a few days later.

Indeed, back-to-back national titles had its privileges on the recruiting trail that even the biggest truckload of NIL money couldn't buy. After UConn's visit to the White House in September 2024, Dan Hurley and his entire staff drove roughly 30 minutes down the road to see 7-foot recruit Eric Reibe at the Bullis School in Potomac, Maryland. Hurley, still bedecked in jacket and tie from his latest visit with President Biden, made quite an impression on Reibe that day.

Around a month later, the big man committed to the Huskies over Indiana, Creighton, Kansas, and others, hoping to become the next Donovan Clingan.

In the moments after the win over Purdue, associate head coach Kimani Young and assistants Luke Murray and Tom Moore all quickly affirmed they would return to UConn. Numerous times over the prior few years, Hurley had beat the drum that Young and Murray, in particular, would make great head coaches somewhere and was miffed that they weren't getting many opportunities.

Of course, Hurley made sure they were among the most well-paid assistants in the country, and he obviously benefited from their loyalty to the program.

But it remained to be seen which players would return to Storrs for a potential three-peat. Tristen Newton and Cam Spencer had exhausted their eligibility. Clingan and Stephon Castle were projected NBA Draft lottery picks and quickly entered the draft process.

Karaban was the biggest question mark. He, too, entered the NBA Draft process, taking advantage of a relatively new rule that allowed underclassmen to explore their options, get feedback from NBA front office people and scouts through workouts and interviews, and ultimately have the chance to decide to return to school or stay in the draft by around Memorial Day.

For about 11 months of the year, it was "we season" at UConn, Hurley liked to say. For this month or so, it was "me season." Players had to do what was best for them.

Karaban was an interesting case. He had arrived at UConn in January 2022 but sat out the second half of the season as a redshirt. Karaban was on the bench for UConn's opening game the following season, but wound up getting 29 minutes of run after Samson Johnson suffered an injury that wound up keeping him out of action for more than a month.

Karaban would never again begin a game in which he played on the bench, starting the next 77 games over two championship seasons. He averaged 9.3 points per game as a freshman while shooting 40.2 percent from three-point range, then 13.2 points per game as a sophomore, though his 3-point percentage dipped to a still respectable 37.9 percent.

And yet somehow, someway, individual honors had curiously eluded Karaban. He was beaten out by Villanova's Cam Whitmore for Big East Freshman of the Year, which still irks Hurley to this day.

Through the 2023 NCAA tournament run and the 2024 Big East tourney run, Adama Sanogo, Tristen Newton, and Donovan Clingan had all garnered various Most Outstanding Player awards.

As the confetti fell from the rafters at State Farm Stadium following the Huskies' second straight national title, the all-tournament team appeared on the videoboard: Newton, Clingan, Stephon Castle, Cam Spencer, and . . . Zach Edey.

Once again, no Karaban, the only one of UConn's five starters not to be honored.

Ultimately, of course, Karaban boasted the best hardware of all.

"I'd rather win national championships," he said. "Obviously, I wouldn't trade that for the world."

In mid-May 2024, UConn secured yet another amazing feat: all five of the Huskies' starters were invited to the NBA Draft combine at Chicago's Wintrust Arena. Remarkable, really.

While all five players had plenty to gain (or lose) during drills, interviews, and five-on-five scrimmages in front of NBA personnel, Karaban was the only one still weighing whether to stay in the draft or chase history at UConn.

He certainly gave the NBA something to think about over the weeklong stay in Chicago. During 3-point shooting drills on Monday, Karaban finished first among the more than 70 NBA prospects in three different shooting drills, knocking down a remarkable 69 out of 81 three-pointers in those respective drills.

In a five-on-five scrimmage the next day, Karaban missed all four of his 3s. But the day after, he bounced back with 12 points on 4-for-5 shooting, including a 3-pointer.

All five UConn players performed pretty well at the combine. Clingan and Castle eschewed the five-on-five scrimmages, as most prospective lottery picks do. Nothing really to gain there.

On the advice of his agent, Newton, no lock to even be drafted, surprisingly skipped the scrimmages as well.

"The past two years have been good for me," he reasoned. "We feel like the film speaks for itself."

Karaban and Cam Spencer took no such risks. Later in the week, Karaban conducted interviews with various NBA teams, then flew out for workouts over the next couple of weeks.

He wrestled with the decision, getting feedback from his family, his coaches, and his agents. He was seen as a possible late first-round pick, possibly a second-round pick . . . or possibly not drafted at all (like Adama Sanogo the year before) and at the whim of signing with a team as an undrafted free agent.

On the morning of May 28, 2024, the last day Karaban had to make a decision, he still wasn't sure what to do.

"He woke up 50–50," his mom, Olga, reported.

Ultimately, at around 2:30 p.m., Karaban posted a message on social media.

"While I've enjoyed the draft process, Storrs is home. Let's run it back."

Just like that, UConn had one of the top returning players in the country back in the fold to chase a near-unprecedented third straight national championship. The only other program to accomplish that feat was John Wooden's UCLA teams, which won a remarkable seven straight titles behind Lew Alcindor, Bill Walton, Keith Wilkes, and Gail Goodrich & Co. from 1967 to 1973.

"It took a lot of thinking, but it makes sense for Alex," Olga Karaban said. "He wants to make history again."

Karaban's stated goal was to be a first-round draft pick. With that hardly guaranteed, another year at UConn as the team's captain and leader, perhaps another national title, would certainly improve those odds for 2025.

And so, Alex Karaban was back in the fold. So were two-time champions Hassan Diarra and Samson Johnson, both in line to start after spending the prior two seasons as key players off the bench.

The "Fab Five" was back, except for Castle, who became the program's first one-and-done freshman since Andre Drummond in 2012. Solo Ball, Jaylin Stewart, and Jayden Ross all figured to have much bigger roles as sophomores. And the recruiting was still humming along.

Ahmad Nowell, a tough, burly, four-star point guard from Philadelphia, and Isaiah Abraham, a long, athletic, defensive-minded forward from Virginia, had already committed.

And at the end of April, UConn nabbed the crown jewel of its 2024 recruiting class. Liam McNeeley, a five-star forward and teammate/friend of Cooper Flagg at national powerhouse Montverde Academy in Florida, had backed out of his commitment to Indiana in March. The Huskies swooped in, ultimately landing the 6-foot-7, McDonald's All-American—the Huskies' second "Burger Boy" in a row, following Castle a year prior.

The Huskies were losing a lot of talent. Stephon Castle was taken by San Antonio with the No. 4 overall pick of the 2024 NBA Draft. Clingan got selected three picks later by Portland (ironically, where he had done some of his best work as a freshman at the Phil Knight Invitational in November 2022). In the second round, Tristen Newton, Mr. Triple-Double himself, went No. 49 overall to Indiana. And Cam Spencer was selected at No. 53 by Detroit, then quickly traded to Memphis.

The four NBA Draft picks were the most for UConn since that 2006 team that had five selections (four first-rounders) after getting popped by George Mason in the Elite Eight. Still, the Huskies had some prime talent returning and/or joining the program.

Then, out of nowhere, UConn was hit with the possibility of losing its most important figure of all.

32

Say Goodbye to Hollywood

A day in the life of Dan Hurley can be a whirlwind of intersecting emotions and oddities: self-deprecation and self-assuredness, introspection and superstitions, lucky underwear and burning sage.

Now imagine Hurley in the eye of a five-day hurricane that included life-altering decisions, wild rumors, national headlines, and, somehow, a strange amalgam of Billy Joel, LeBron James, Magic Johnson, and Jimmy Kimmel.

Such was Hurley's world in early June 2024, when the Los Angeles Lakers made a strong bid to pluck the two-time defending national champion coach from UConn and make him their new head coach.

"It was total madness," Hurley would later tell *CT Insider*.

It also wasn't the first time Hurley had been wooed by one of basketball's most hallowed franchises. On the eve of the national championship game against Purdue, reports surfaced that Hurley was being targeted by perennial national powerhouse Kentucky to take over its blue-blood program. John Calipari had decided to leave the program after 15 seasons, including the 2012 national championship season, to take over the reins at Southeastern Conference rival Arkansas.

Hurley was seen as Calipari's perfect replacement, but he quickly shot down those rumors after the Huskies finished off Purdue.

"Yeah, I don't think that's a concern," Hurley said in the glow of a second straight national title. "My wife, you should have her answer that. She'll answer that question better than I can."

There was no chance that Andrea Hurley, the ultimate "Jersey Girl" ("I channel my inner Jackie Kennedy, but I can go to Snooki in five seconds"), was leaving the East Coast for Lexington, Kentucky.

Maybe the Lakers were a different story.

Hurley had signed a six-year, $32.5 million extension with UConn in June 2023. A second straight title compelled the school to tear that up and come up with a new one. On Wednesday, June 5, Hurley told reporters at a UConn Coaches' Road Show in Stamford, Connecticut, that negotiations for a new contract had "probably taken more time than any of us would have liked."

Eyebrows were slightly raised.

The following morning, ESPN's Adrian Wojnarowski, a close confidant of the Hurley family, reported that Lakers vice president of basketball operations Rob Pelinka and owner Jeanie Buss were eager to hire Hurley for the job vacated by recently fired Darvin Ham.

This really raised eyebrows throughout the sports world.

Once that news broke, Hurley addressed his team in a meeting.

"I didn't like the way they looked at me when I told them I was going to consider it," he later reported.

Hurley flew out to Los Angeles that night and met with Pelinka and Buss the next day. Back home, UConn fans worried that their beloved coach might be gone after just six short (and immensely successful) seasons. Hurley had said several times, after all, that he would welcome the challenge of someday coaching an NBA team.

Longtime NBA journalists and uninformed podcasters alike opined that Hurley was simply using the Lakers as leverage to try to pry more money from UConn in a new contract. Others thought he wouldn't be able to turn down the Lakers' offer, which several sources believed would be worth $100 million over multiple years.

Magic Johnson, perhaps the greatest Laker of all, went on *Jimmy Kimmel Live* and professed his desire to have Hurley take over the team. A two-month-old Twitter post from Laker star LeBron James that praised Hurley's offensive schemes ("he's so DAMN GOOD!") went viral.

"Even if you're not on social media, you may just walk by a TV and they're talking about it on FS1, on ESPN," Hurley recalled. "Your phone's blowing up. You're thinking about the situation, too. About what you want to do while everyone else is just speculating nonstop about it."

By Saturday night, Hurley was back on the East Coast. And when assistant coach Luke Murray posted a short video of Murray and Dan and Andrea Hurley enjoying a Billy Joel concert at Madison Square Garden, the consensus was that Hurley had said goodbye to Hollywood and was coming back to UConn.

Would Andrea want to uproot to the West Coast? For that matter, with his parents still in New Jersey and able to drive to most of his games, Dan Hurley probably wouldn't want to leave the East Coast, either.

And what about his players? What about Alex Karaban, who just a couple of weeks earlier had pulled out of the NBA Draft process at the last minute to go for a third straight national title with Hurley? What about Liam McNeeley, who had recently committed to Hurley, expecting to play for him?

No possible way Hurley would leave all of that for La La Land, right?

Right. On Monday morning, Hurley announced to his team, then to the world, that he was staying put.

"My whole mindset, the type of coaching that suits me best right now, is certainly college," Hurley told *CT Insider*. "I want to be able to control my own destiny the best that I can. I schedule my games, I pick the players, I hire the staff, I decide how long we're going to practice, when we're going to practice."

He wasn't going to get that kind of autonomy in Los Angeles, where LeBron seemed to pull the strings so much that the Lakers drafted his son, Bronny, in the second round, even though he had averaged just 4.8 points per game in his one season at USC.

The fact that the Lakers' ultimate offer of six years, $70 million, while more than UConn could pay him, was far less than the $100 million figure bandied about, probably was a factor as well. UConn wound up giving him a new, six-year, $50 million pact, making him the second-highest-paid coach in college basketball after Kansas' Bill Self.

In the span of a few months, Dan Hurley had rebuffed offers from two of the most prestigious franchises in all of basketball: the Los Angeles Lakers and the University of Kentucky. That certainly can't hurt in pitches to prospects on the recruiting trail.

But there was one other major factor behind Hurley's decision: history. The 2024–2025 Huskies had the chance to become the first (and only) three-peat national champion since John Wooden's UCLA teams from 1967 to 1973. Bob Hurley Sr. was a John Wooden disciple, and Dan has the ultimate respect for Wooden, calling him "the founding father of coaches."

In April 2025, Hurley would have the chance to join John Wooden's elite company. Not bad for a guy who, just 15 years earlier, was making about $45,000 a year as coach/history teacher at St. Benedict's Prep, driving the team bus to games.

"To do something that hasn't been done since the '70s, and now there's two more rounds in the [NCAA] tournament," Hurley said, before pausing to shake his head in wonderment. "The UCLA program is the biggest ever in college, and [Wooden] is the greatest coach. So, there's a lot of motivation."

The Huskies had lost a lot of talent. But then, they had the year before, as well, and bounced back even better. In the Big East, Creighton had 7-footer Ryan Kalkbrenner returning for a fifth season. Villanova had Eric Dixon back for a sixth. Marquette had eight of its rotation players back. Rick Pitino had reloaded at St. John's through the transfer portal.

Nationally, teams like Alabama, Auburn, Duke, Gonzaga, Houston, Kansas, North Carolina, and Florida looked strong.

But UConn's toughest rival for the upcoming season wasn't going to be Ryan Kalkbrenner or Eric Dixon, Bill Self or Rick Pitino, Hunter

Dickinson or Cooper Flagg, or Creighton, Kansas, or Carolina. It would be a program based in Los Angeles but not the Lakers.

UConn's toughest rival for the season would be UCLA. John Wooden's UCLA. Lew Alcindor, Bill Walton, Jamaal Wilkes, and Gail Goodrich. The ghosts of UCLA past.

UConn's biggest rival in 2024–2025 would be history.

33

Wooden Dreams

Dan Hurley and John Wooden.

The Jersey Boy and the Wizard of Westwood.

As the 2024–2025 season neared, did the two belong in the same sentence yet? Maybe not. Hurley had won two national titles, back-to-back. Wooden won 10 national titles, a record seven in a row. In that stretch, he once won 88 straight games.

There's a reason why the award given to the most outstanding men's and women's college basketball players each year is named the Wooden Award.

Dan Hurley hadn't reached that level yet. Except in one small East Coast enclave.

"We say here in Jersey City, regularly: 'John Wooden and Danny. How about that?'" Hurley's father, Bob Sr., told *CT Insider*.

And if Hurley were able to lead the Huskies to a third straight national title, he would solely be in the company of Wooden—at least in men's basketball. Indeed, Hurley need only walk down the hall at the Werth Family Champions Center and seek out a man who won more national titles than even Wooden.

Geno Auriemma had led the UConn women's team to 11 national championships entering the 2024–2025 season, including four in a row at one point, three in a row at another. Growing up in suburban Philadelphia, Auriemma was a huge fan of Wooden. While guiding the

UConn women to those 11 titles in the span of 21 seasons, he often heard his name linked with the Wizard of Westwood.

"I didn't necessarily appreciate the comparison," Auriemma recalled, "because it was different from UCLA."

Wooden built his dynasty on his "Pyramid of Success," with adages like "Don't mistake activity for accomplishment" and "Perception meets opportunity."

"At the end of the day," Auriemma noted, "I'm more practical in that sense that the 'Pyramid of Success' is Diana [Taurasi], Maya [Moore], Stewie [Breanna Stewart], Tina Charles, Rebecca [Lobo], Nykesha [Sales] . . . that's the pyramid. That's how you build it."

Of course, Wooden often had his pick of the top recruits in the country back in the 1960s and early 1970s. He got Lew Alcindor (later Kareem Abdul-Jabbar) to come across the country to Westwood from New York City, eager to play at the school where his hero, Jackie Robinson, had played. He got Bill Walton to make the much shorter trip up from San Diego.

Bob Knight, another all-time great coach and three-time national champion, often accused Wooden of having used somewhat illicit recruiting tactics. But that's another story, another book.

UConn never really had the advantage of attracting the best of the best recruits. Even three-time national champion Jim Calhoun brought in only a small handful of McDonald's All-Americans over his 26 seasons at the helm, instead relying on a steady stream of national top-30 and top-50 recruits, mixed with some three- or four-year projects, and developing it all into championship contention.

Hurley believed in the same philosophy. Kentucky, Duke, North Carolina, and Kansas (the so-called "blue bloods") had their pick of the nation's top recruits. Most of these players ended up as "one-and-dones"—play one requisite year of college, then head to the NBA. It led to a lot of wins, but not necessarily to a lot of championships: Kentucky's John Calipari won just one title, in 2012, behind one-and-done center Anthony Davis.

Of course, the advent of the NCAA transfer portal, which was now allowing players to transfer almost at will and not have to sit out a year, and name, image, and likeness (NIL) money, which was paying some athletes six- or seven-figure salaries, had changed everything over the prior few years.

Hurley didn't like it. He much preferred building a program from the ground up, recruiting players who fit his mold out of high school to develop over two, three, four years, and augment that with the occasional transfer or two to fill some needs.

And, for the most part, that's what Hurley had done over his first six years at UConn. Prior to the 2021–2022 season, UConn was one of only a handful of "Power Six" teams not to take in a single player through the portal. But it should be noted that Hurley's two top scorers on the 2023–2024 national championship team, Tristen Newton and Cam Spencer, were both transfers. Hurley had also hit big on transfers like R. J. Cole, Tyrese Martin, and Joey Calcaterra, and he was hoping for similar results in 2024–2025 from Tarris Reed Jr. (Michigan) and Aidan Mahaney (Saint Mary's).

Still, Hurley was recruiting high school players at a high level. Stephon Castle (2024) and Liam McNeeley (2025) were back-to-back McDonald's All-Americans in a program that hadn't had one since Alterique Gilbert in 2016, under Kevin Ollie. Prior to that, it was Alex Oriakhi in 2009, under Calhoun.

"Even the programs that have the most advantages, the programs that get the first crack in recruiting, have had a great difficulty winning championships [since the mid-2000s]," Hurley pointed out. "I think the game nowadays [is harder]. Obviously the portal, NIL, losing early-entry players to the NBA, as well as the game has gotten way more complex at the college level, because there are so many different styles of play that you play against nowadays, whether it's teams that play zone or switching man or the 'pack' line or the ball-pressure man. And all the unique styles of play as an offense that you face as a college coach. We don't have the rules that force you to play defense a certain way."

Added Auriemma, "He's gone out and got the kids out of the portal that fit his culture, his program and philosophy. And he's been able to get really good high school players to come in and coach them up. So, he's kind of got the daily double there."

Of course, Hurley had another motivating factor: the lack of respect he felt he and his program continued to get from the national media. And when the 2024–2025 preseason Associated Press Top 25 men's basketball poll was released on October 14, 2024, Hurley had more ammunition.

UConn was picked No. 3 in the inaugural poll. Kansas was No. 1, Alabama No. 2.

"I don't understand how we just don't start the season [at No. 1]," Hurley said after UConn's 102–75 romp over Rhode Island in an exhibition game that night at Mohegan Sun Arena. "Not that it matters, because you've got to do it. But we dominate for the [2023] national championship, we lose all the players, and then we're even better [in 2023–2024]. We dominate even more, we lose all the players . . . I think we should've been voted first."

In fact, Hurley had told a podcast earlier in the offseason that he felt the Huskies should be a "consensus" No. 1.

"Whether we are, legitimately, the No. 1 team . . . I think it would've been better for eyeballs on college, story lines, attention, rewarding a program that's dominated like no one has in a very long time," Hurley said. "We're not gonna harp on it. Being ranked third compared to one . . . it's not like they ranked us 12th. And there are a lot of question marks with the team, we acknowledge that. But there were a lot of question marks the last two years, too."

At least one thing had changed. A little over a week later, UConn was a unanimous choice among Big East coaches to finish first. Alex Karaban was (finally!) preseason first-team All–Big East. Aidan Mahaney was (surprisingly) a third-team selection. Liam McNeeley was preseason Freshman of the Year.

But once again, Karaban received a snub. Creighton's Ryan Kalkbrenner was named preseason Player of the Year.

Either way, No. 3 or No. 1 or No. 12, UConn was about to kick off a run at history. The chase for John Wooden was on.

No one could have imagined what a grueling, exhausting, and, ultimately, frustrating chase it would be for Dan Hurley and the Huskies.

34

Official Problems

Back on that New Year's Eve 2023 game in Cincinnati against Xavier, the precipice of UConn's January of discontent, Dan Hurley was hit with a key technical foul late in the game that put UConn behind the eight-ball and, ultimately, may have cost the Huskies a victory.

And if that scenario sounded familiar, it's because nearly the exact same thing had happened the *prior* February, in the same building, when a Hurley "T" with 3:49 left to play helped turn a five-point UConn deficit into seven in an eventual 74–68 loss.

After that game, he publicly lambasted the officiating, particularly Doug Shows, who hit Hurley with the "T" after the coach had argued about a foul called by a different official on Tyrese Martin.

"I don't know where Doug came from there, he came flying in, obviously," Hurley told reporters. "I watch a lot of games, and I'm at a lot of my games, and I see a lot of coaches in the ear of officials. I don't think there was anything there that warranted a technical. So, I'll be calling up our head of officials, because I want an explanation on that."

"And it's such a potentially bad call," the coach added. "Running in when somebody's made a call that's potentially bad, and then call a borderline technical, is not good officiating."

Hurley also said the two fouls called on center Adama Sanogo within the game's first 5½ minutes were "brutal calls . . . a joke."

Even worse, while Hurley was talking to a couple of reporters outside the visitors' locker room a few minutes later, the officials left their own locker room and walked by. One official waved at Hurley and appeared to try to say something.

"Don't say shit to me!" Hurley barked back. "No waves! I'm not waving!"

The next day, Hurley was publicly admonished by the Big East Conference.

"Big East sportsmanship rules prohibit our coaches from public criticism of our game officials," the league said in a statement. "We have established protocols in place for feedback by our schools regarding any officiating matter, and while we understand that tensions run high during the season, we expect these protocols to be honored."

In an accompanying statement, UConn said it was in "full support" of the Big East's admonishment. There was no fine, no suspension.

Of course, less than two weeks later, Hurley was ejected in the first half from that Villanova game in Hartford. Kimani Young took over and guided the Huskies to their first win over the Wildcats in eight years.

Nearly a year later, on New Year's Eve, Hurley was in almost the exact same position at Xavier, picking up a technical foul with 2:25 left that helped turn a four-point deficit into six in an eventual 83–73 loss to the Musketeers.

Hurley simply had to tone it down. His passion and intensity had got him to where he was, one of the best coaches (if not *the* best) in college basketball. But he couldn't keep costing his team games.

Sure, officials make some bad calls and sometimes need to have thicker skin. But Hurley had to realize that he may not have built up a reservoir of goodwill with the referees, either. They're human, after all.

Hurley had a long history of sniping with refs, beginning with that ejection from a closed-door scrimmage while at Rhode Island. In a January 2023 win at Villanova, Hurley was caught on camera calling referee Jeffrey Anderson "a f—king clown."

But he noted that, once his teams started getting better, his sideline demeanor improved as well. That was the case at URI, he noted.

Hurley was ejected from two of his first 18 games at UConn in 2018–2019, against Syracuse at Madison Square Garden in just his third game, and that double-ejection with Frank Haith on a cold night in Tulsa. Those Husky teams weren't very good.

As UConn got better, Hurley's antics toned down a bit, for a while. But then came Xavier, Villanova, and Xavier again.

And then came back-to-back national championships, which would seem to have calmed down Hurley even more. But that's not how he's wired.

UConn opened up its 2024–2025 campaign with its usual array of "buy games" against weak-sister, low-major programs. The Huskies beat a "Murderer's Row" of Sacred Heart, New Hampshire, Le Moyne, and East Texas A&M by an average of nearly 38 points per game. But they attempted just five more free throws than those opponents and committed just four fewer fouls.

Le Moyne, a program that had made the transition to Division I only a year earlier, committed fewer fouls (10) than UConn (13) in Hartford. East Texas A&M, a school that had just changed its *name* a few weeks earlier, traipsed to the line 22 times on November 19, 2024, at Gampel Pavilion—eight more times than the two-time defending national champs!

"Inconceivable," Hurley said after the game.

For Hurley, it all came down to a lack of respect he felt a two-time national champion program deserved.

"I just remember what it was like to play Villanova, when I was a low-major coach," he noted. "When you went on the road and played a 'buy' game, what that experience was like. I played the Duke teams with Coach K, and I'm not comparing myself to these coaches, but Jay Wright, when [Villanova was] on top of the sport, I remember how tough it was to get a 60/40 call for me, or a 70/30 call for me. Never mind a continuation call."

In fact, Hurley harked way back to November 14, 2011, when he brought Wagner into Gampel to face Jim Calhoun and the defending national-champion, No. 4-ranked Huskies.

Wagner went to the foul line 17 times. UConn? The Huskies went to the foul line 43 times. UConn was whistled for 18 fouls, Wagner for 28.

"Matter of fact," Hurley recalled, "the referees wouldn't even talk to me [in that game]."

That said, UConn was now 4–0 to start the 2024–2025 season. After Alabama dropped an early-season game to Purdue, UConn sent out an email to AP Top 25 voters asking them to consider voting UConn No. 1 that week, a move seemingly beneath a two-time national-champion program. It didn't work, as Kansas remained at No. 1, but the Huskies jumped to No. 2 in the AP poll.

Now, the Huskies were off to tropical Hawaii, where a top-notch Maui Invitational field awaited.

And where Dan Hurley's relationship with officials was about to hit a new low.

35

Mayhem in Maui

Dan Hurley isn't really a beach guy. Jersey Shore, sure. He vacations there with family each summer. But the tropical beaches of Hawaii, with pineapples and luaus and Hawaiian shirts? Not really his scene. At all.

That was rather evident from the time UConn flew into Maui on Friday, November 22, 2024. On Saturday, the team went over film and scouting and practiced at Lahaina Civic Center. Afterward, most of the team went on a jet-skiing excursion. Most of the players, that is. None of the coaches. Certainly not the head coach.

"I watched film," Hurley reported, matter-of-factly.

On Sunday morning, the tournament's eight coaches took part in a press conference at the Hyatt Regency hotel. Bedecked in a Hawaiian shirt and a lei, Hurley couldn't have looked more out of place—a Jersey City kid against the backdrop of sand, surfboards, and the Pacific Ocean.

The coaches then competed in a foul-shooting contest, where each was paired with a local elementary school kid and shot three foul shots apiece on an eight-foot net. Hurley made his first shot off the back rim, eliciting an "Ohh" from a couple of spectators.

"Stop moaning," he said to the fans, seemingly jokingly, as he hoisted up his second shot. A miss. He then swished his third shot, confidently walking away while the ball was in midair.

Hurley's elementary school partner knocked down all three of his shots, giving the duo the victory, yet another one for Hurley.

It was Hurley's last victory of the week.

Later that afternoon, Hurley met with a couple of Connecticut reporters in the Hyatt lobby. He spoke quietly, choosing his words carefully, seemingly sensing something ominous coming. The Huskies were slated to play Memphis on Monday, but Hurley wasn't sure if his team was ready. UConn's staff had privately been a bit miffed that the two-time defending champs would draw such a tough, opening-game opponent (there's that lack of respect again), but Hurley said that it wasn't a concern. He did seem a bit miffed by the 9:30 a.m. starting time, however.

"We've got to be the more-ready team at 9:30 a.m.," he said.

The Huskies weren't. Hurley might argue the refs weren't, either.

Just over 4 minutes into the game, UConn's mild-mannered trainer James Doran, of all people, was hit with a technical foul.

"A trainer who is just the nicest guy, a very quiet guy, might have muttered something under his breath," Hurley explained. "Normally in that situation, an official comes over to you and says, 'Hey, Coach, tell that guy to shut up.' Because I know they don't want to hear it from me. That's commonly how that should have been handled. But I had a lot of issues with what went on out there."

UConn found itself down 13 points to the Tigers with 4 minutes to play. But the Huskies staged an impressive comeback, capped by Solo Ball's 3-pointer with 1.2 seconds left that sent the game to overtime.

That's where things really got crazy.

Three technical fouls were called in the five-minute extra session, including a crucial one on Hurley. With 40.3 seconds left in overtime and the game tied at 92, Liam McNeeley was called for an over-the-back foul. Hurley disagreed vehemently, dramatically falling to the floor on the sidelines.

"That was a joke," Hurley said of the foul call. "There was no attempt to block out. There was a player on Memphis that made a half-assed effort to rebound that basketball, and Liam McNeeley high-pointed that rebound. For that call to be made, at that point of the game, was a complete joke."

Hurley was hit with the technical for his wild sideline reaction.

"I don't know what happened. I might have lost my balance by the absurdity of the call. Or, maybe I tripped. But if I made that call, at that point, I would've ignored the fact that I was on my back."

PJ Carter hit four straight free throws, and Memphis held on for a 99–97 win.

Aloha, UConn's 17-game winning streak, which dated back to that February 20, 2024, loss at Creighton. UConn had been 47–3 since December 2023.

Memphis nearly doubled up the Huskies in free-throw attempts, 40–24. Samson Johnson fouled out of the game after picking up an unnecessary technical foul with 2½ minutes left in overtime.

"He's got to be smarter," Hurley said of the senior center. "But Samson was getting shoved, his jersey was ripped. He didn't get a foul called for him the entire game; he ended the game with his jersey ripped down the center and he didn't get a single call. He's frustrated."

So was Hurley. And his sideline antics and technical were blared all over sports news stations the rest of the day.

"The difference really is the technical foul on Dan Hurley," said Jay Bilas, who called the game for ESPN.

"The technical by Danny Hurley really changed the game," added ESPN's Dalen Cuff.

Hurley told CBSSports.com that he didn't believe his technical cost UConn the game.

"I think it was the shitty calls," he said. "I don't know too many back-to-back national championship teams that get that type of a whistle."

In truth, Hurley had been sniping at the officials throughout the game and probably could have been called for a technical at least two or three other times. And several national college basketball analysts were calling him out on it.

Even ESPN's Seth Greenberg, a confidant of Hurley's who lives in Connecticut and attends several Husky practices, was critical.

"Unfortunately for UConn, he overreacted," Greenberg said in studio. "He was strung tight a good portion of this game. The officials had enough, they whack him. And in the end, that becomes the difference in the game."

UConn fell into the event's loser's bracket and drew Colorado the following day (this time at 10:30 a.m.), when Hurley would learn the hard way that one ref's over-the-back call is another ref's clean, offensive rebound.

With about 25 seconds left in a tight game, and nearly 24 hours after Liam McNeeley had been called for that over-the-back foul that set off Hurley's "T," Colorado's Trevor Baskin grabbed an offensive rebound over (you guessed it) McNeeley to keep the Buffalos' possession alive. No foul was called, much to Hurley's disagreement.

After a time-out, Colorado's Andrej Jakimovski hit a tough runner with 8 seconds left to put Colorado up for good in a 73–72 victory.

"It just speaks to how these last two games have gone for us," Hurley said. "[Monday], the biggest play of the game was an over-the-back that was called against us. [Tuesday], it was more egregious because Baskin pulled Liam's arm down. I saw the replay of it. It's ironic."

Don't ya think?

For the second straight game, UConn's main big men, Samson Johnson and Tarris Reed Jr., fouled out. UConn committed eight more fouls (22–14) than Colorado and shot just 13 free throws to the Buffalos' 28.

Hurley seemed to pull his punches a bit when asked about the foul discrepancy and officiating. He was clearly frustrated but not only with the refs.

"Our defense has been so dreadful out here. We had opportunities. It's been a tough two days."

One more day remained, and UConn would have to wait through nearly all of it to tip off in its final bout in Maui against Dayton. The game was slated for a 7 p.m. local tip-off—midnight, back in Connecticut. UConn would begin its Thanksgiving Day in the wee hours, playing a game some 5,000 miles from home.

Perhaps it was a good thing that this game started so late back home. UConn turned in one of its worst performances in years.

Dayton blitzed the Huskies practically from the start, shot 47 percent from the three-point line and outrebounded UConn 41–25 in an 85–67 victory.

The two-time defending champion Huskies began the week No. 2 in the nation and ended it No. 8 in an eight-team tournament. It was their first three-game losing streak since that awful January of 2023.

"It was a humbling trip," Hurley said, in a massive understatement.

To make matters worse, Alex Karaban suffered a concussion late in the game and had to be transported to a hospital near the other side of the island. Karaban, UConn's leading scorer and team captain, was fouled while driving to the basket with about 2½ minutes left and hit his head on the floor. He went to the foul line, hit one of two shots, and remained in the game. But after the game ended, he felt woozy and was put in concussion protocol and sent for a CT scan.

With UConn set to fly home that night, there was a serious chance that Karaban would have to stay back in Maui for an extra night or two (joined by at least one or two members of the Huskies' staff).

Fortunately, Karaban was ultimately cleared to make the flight home just before takeoff. And that was a good thing in more ways than one. No one on UConn wanted to stay an extra minute in Maui. Certainly not Hurley.

Once again, UConn was outshot badly from the foul line, 30–11. The Huskies were whistled for 21 fouls, Dayton just 13.

Over the three games at Maui, UConn's opponents took 50 more free throws than the Huskies: 98–48. That was something Hurley would mention frequently moving forward.

But it wasn't all the refs. UConn was not defending well, particularly from the three-point line. Memphis, Colorado, and Dayton (all unranked heading into the tournament) combined to hit 29 three-pointers at an impressive 53 percent rate.

"Right now," Hurley said, shortly before boarding the bus to the airport for the long trip home, "we're a shell of what we've been."

36

Return to the Mainland

"Maui" had overtaken "January" as a nasty word in UConn's vocabulary. After the team's perfunctory, 99–45 whipping of lowly Maryland–Eastern Shore just a couple of days after returning to Connecticut, reporters asked Hurley what he had learned from the Maui experience.

"I'm not doing another three-game MTE (multi-team event)," he replied. "Moving forward, we will only play home-and-home games or single-game events . . . I don't think I'll ever do a three-game MTE again. There's zero chance I ever do that again."

Hurley drew scorching criticism throughout both social and standard media as a whiner who couldn't handle it when things weren't going his way. In truth, the plans for UConn to bow out of future events like Maui or the Battle 4 Atlantis in the Bahamas had been hatched months in advance.

"We're evaluating our scheduling model," UConn athletic director David Benedict told *CT Insider* about a week before Maui. "Just like everything else we're doing, we're trying to identify the most efficient way, financially, to take advantage of the content that we have to create revenue."

And maximizing revenue was particularly important, with name, image, and likeness (NIL) already ruling the land and revenue sharing on the horizon for both current and former athletes, via a recent $2.8 billion House versus NCAA settlement.

Simply put, UConn was spending a lot of money to charter a plane and fly 5,000 miles to Maui, without getting much in return, at least financially. The UConn program did have some great memories in Maui, winning the tournament in 2005 on a Denham Brown buzzer-beater, and again in 2011 behind three straight incredible performances by Kemba Walker. But trophies don't pay bills.

"I think some of these promoters have been doing well off of the backs of some really high-level programs," Benedict noted. "Let's face it, Maui has been the standard for a long time. But, those types of events probably aren't going to be as important as they used to be, because of how the model is changing."

But that was for the future. As for the present, some changes clearly had to be made, and fast. On December 4, 2024, 15th-ranked Baylor was coming to town in the latest and final installment of the Big East/Big 12 Battle.

UConn had fallen from No. 2 in the nation to No. 25 after the three losses in Maui, just barely hanging on to a national ranking. Karaban was ruled out not only for the win over Maryland–Eastern Shore but also for the Baylor game, giving Jaylin Stewart his first two starts as a collegian.

Hurley had made another lineup change that had nothing to do with injury. Back in Maui, Hurley moved veteran Hassan Diarra into the starting lineup as point guard. Diarra was the Big East's Sixth Man Award winner the year before, a perfect boost of energy and defense off the bench to spell Tristen Newton or Stephon Castle. Hurley figured Diarra could provide similar contributions this season, albeit with more playing time.

Aidan Mahaney, the transfer from Saint Mary's, began the season as the starting point guard, but it just wasn't working. Mahaney was more of a shooter, averaging exactly 13.9 points per game in both his freshman and sophomore seasons at Saint Mary's.

But Mahaney wasn't a fit as UConn's de facto starting point guard. He struggled to find Samson Johnson for lobs or Karaban and Solo Ball for open 3-pointers. He struggled to play downhill and drive to the basket very effectively. Worst of all, he struggled mightily on defense, though he was hardly alone on the team in that category.

And so, after the loss to Memphis in Maui, Hurley switched Diarra to starting point guard against Colorado. As if on cue, Diarra hit Johnson with a lob dunk to start the Huskies' scoring. He finished with 11 points, 6 assists, and 3 turnovers in that game, then 10 points, 5 assists, and 1 turnover against Dayton.

Obviously, the team's results weren't great, with two more losses. But Diarra continued to play well as UConn returned to the mainland. He had 11 assists in wins at Texas and against Xavier, 9 assists at DePaul and at Villanova, and 8 assists to go with a career-high 19 points in a comeback win over Providence.

Meanwhile, he didn't turn the ball over more than three times in any of 12 straight games. Diarra was never going to be a great shooter or a prolific scorer, but he was providing exactly what Hurley wanted from his point guard: ball distribution, security, and leadership.

"It probably would have made more sense to start him from the opener," Hurley confessed after the Providence game. "Just have him at the natural point guard position, rather than to put a square peg in a round hole there with trying to force that on Aidan.

"I screwed up the early part of the season there."

Meanwhile, Mahaney looked much more comfortable in his bench role. He popped in a season-best 15 points in that win over Providence, and he made nice contributions in wins over Butler and Baylor.

Ah yes, back to Baylor. With Karaban out, others had to step up against the Bears. Liam McNeeley led the way with 17 points and 8 rebounds, but it was Samson Johnson who was "an incredible warrior," per Hurley.

The senior center was near-perfect on offense, scoring a season-high 13 points on 4-for-4 shooting from the floor and 5-for-6 from the foul line. He blocked a pair of shots and grabbed 4 rebounds, and also paired with fellow 6-foot-10 center Tarris Reed Jr. in a rare double-big look for the Huskies.

Hurley had played Adama Sanogo and Donovan Clingan together for only a few short minutes throughout the 2022–2023 season and never had Clingan and Johnson share the floor in 2023–2024. It worked out pretty well.

But with Karaban out, and Baylor throwing out a big, athletic lineup, Hurley bucked tradition and went double-big. Reed added 9 points and 5 rebounds, and it all added up to a 76–72 Husky victory in Hartford.

It was a relief for Hurley, who admitted he had had some "sleepless nights" after Maui, envisioning a scenario where the Huskies could lose their next three games (Baylor, at Texas, and versus Gonzaga at Madison Square Garden) and enter Big East play with a losing record.

In fact, the Huskies would do the exact opposite. Later in the week, UConn traveled down to Austin, Texas, to play the Longhorns at Moody Center. It was a sort of homecoming for McNeeley, who grew up in suburban Dallas, a good three hours down the road. He had dozens of family and friends at the game.

But it was Karaban who stole the show. After sitting out the prior two games in concussion protocol ("one of the longest weeks of my life"), Karaban notched a double-double with 21 points and 11 rebounds to lead the Huskies to a 76–65 win.

"I'm just super-excited to be back with the boys," Karaban said after the game. "We're turning stuff around right now."

Indeed, they were.

"Maybe the people with the shovels in the dirt, maybe they were too quick to grab the shovel and throw the dirt on us," Hurley added. "Maybe. We'll see."

The New "Queen of Connecticut"

Andrea Sirakides Hurley is a Jersey girl to the core, growing up in the town of Freehold, then Toms River. Her parents, Ken and Patty, grew up in Jersey City, and Ken used to bring his young daughter to watch St. Anthony's, led by a guard named Dan Hurley, face Christian Brothers Academy each year in a rivalry game.

But since Andrea arrived in Connecticut after her husband took over the UConn job in March 2018, she has become a beloved figure in the state. Her sassy demeanor ("I channel my Jackie Kennedy, but I can go Snooki in five seconds"), passion for her family and the UConn men's basketball team, colorful criticism of other fan bases, and tireless charitable work have earned her the nickname "The Queen of Connecticut" from UConn fans.

For Dan Hurley, she is a wife, best friend, and, quite simply, "the best thing ever to happen to me."

They met, through Andrea's friend, late in Andrea's freshman year at Seton Hall. After a second date, they went back to Dan's apartment, where he turned on the TV to watch golf, opened a package of Ritz crackers, and barely spoke.

Andrea asked him to take her home. Dan got up, went outside, and then came back to inform her that his car had been stolen.

"Are you gonna call the cops?" Andrea asked.

"No, tomorrow."

"Your parents?"

"No, tomorrow."

Andrea slept the whole night sitting up, wearing her shoes and coat the entire time, in case she had to run out of the apartment. And yet . . .

"I kinda liked it," she confesses. "I was like, 'This guy's nuts.'"

They stuck together. A few years later, in August 1997, they got married. It's been a wild, unpredictable ride ever since.

Their first child was due on July 7, 1999, but Dan had to be out recruiting that week. So, Andrea drank a couple of bottles of castor oil, then walked around the neighborhood all day, to induce labor.

Danny Jr. was born on July 1, 1999. Andrew arrived a few years later.

Andrea has never picked up a basketball in her life. She's seen thousands of games but, by her own admission, has "no idea what's going on—nor do I want to."

But at every one of Hurley's stops, from Wagner to Rhode Island to UConn, she's at just about every game. She's also served as the ultimate team mom. Players are always welcome at the Hurleys' Glastonbury home.

"She develops a relationship with these guys that, I think, helps them understand what I'm trying to do more," Dan said. "It improves my relationship with the players."

Her relationship with certain opposing fan bases is . . . not so great. Particularly Providence fans, who she quickly learned not to like while her husband coached at rival Rhode Island.

"I will never go back to that place," she once told the *Field of 68* podcast. "What they did to me there, grown men spitting, throwing beer. That'll never be our fans. Our fans are just hard on the team, which annoys me. But they're not disrespectful."

Andrea promised she'd never again get annoyed by UConn fans, however, after attending the Huskies' first of consecutive national championship parades in April 2023.

"When I saw how many fans we have, and a tiny percentage of fans that are so negative, as opposed to who showed up at that parade . . . it means nothing. The support that this team has is surreal."

While at URI, Andrea began collecting unsold tickets and delivering them to inner-city kids up in Providence and Pawtucket. When she arrived *at UConn, she became deeply involved with the Husky Ticket Project, which raises money to send underprivileged kids to UConn sporting events.*

"She loves getting involved with the community and getting involved in programs," Dan Hurley said, while at a Husky Ticket Project event in September 2023. "People like her a lot more than me, so when she gets in these settings, she makes me look good."

37

Season on the Brink

On December 14, 2024, UConn returned to Madison Square Garden to face No. 7 Gonzaga for the third time in the span of about 20 months. The Zags were led by Ryan Nembhard, who led the nation in assists entering the game at 10.7 per contest, more than 30 NCAA entire *teams* were averaging.

UConn came out on fire with a 13–2 start, powered by a pair of Samson Johnson dunks and an array of McNeeley buckets. UConn hit 6 of its first 7 shots, 8 of its first 11, and 9 of its first 13.

McNeeley wound up the star of the show, finishing with a career-high 26 points in a variety of ways—a 3-pointer off a high bounce off the back iron; flipping in an inside bucket practically over his shoulder.

"I don't know how that one went in," the freshman marveled.

UConn never trailed in the latter half, though the Zags were within five with 23 seconds left and Khalif Battle, who had hit all 33 of his free throws this season, stepping to the line for a pair of foul shots.

He hit the first but missed the second, and UConn had yet another win over Gonzaga. It was the 300th win of Hurley's career.

"UConn, they just have the heart of a champion," mused Zags coach Mark Few, who'd know better than most.

Jaylin Stewart, the Seattle kid who wasn't recruited by hometown Gonzaga, had one of his better games as a Husky, scoring 10 points, half of them kicking off a key, game-changing run midway through the second half.

"They never really showed a lot of interest in me," Stewart said of the Zags, "so I kind of took that a little personally."

The only bad news was that Johnson had suffered a concussion after falling to the floor midway through the first half and would have to miss the Huskies' Big East opener on December 18 against Xavier in Hartford.

The Musketeers had injury issues of their own, most notably 6-foot-9 forward Zach Freemantle, who had missed most of the prior two seasons with foot injuries. He began the 2024–2025 season healthy and playing well, but he had been injured a couple of weeks earlier and was out for the UConn game.

In an absolute classic at XL Center, UConn and Xavier battled back and forth—11 ties and 22 lead changes—and the game extended into overtime. Alex Karaban gave the Huskies the final lead of the game with a 3-pointer 22 seconds into the extra session, and UConn held on for a 94–89 win.

Tarris Reed Jr., Johnson's replacement in the starting lineup, notched a double-double (20 points, 13 rebounds), Solo Ball added 22, and Karaban netted 20 as UConn won a home Big East opener for the first time, remarkably, since 2003.

UConn knocked down 20 of 21 free throws, its only miss a meaningless one with 5 seconds left in overtime by Hassan Diarra. Ironically, Hurley had extended practice by about 25 extra minutes the day before when UConn struggled hitting free throws.

UConn may have won its first home Big East opener in 21 years, but it didn't come without some struggles. The Huskies' season-long issues guarding the three-point line nearly caught up with them, allowing Xavier to knock down 8 of 10 three-pointers in the second half and 13 of 24 for the game.

Granted, some of the 3-pointers hit by Ryan Conwell, Dante Maddox Jr., and Marcus Foster were long, tough shots, with defenders in their face. Ryan Daly–like, or Teddy Allen–like, at times.

"I actually didn't think our 3-point defense was that bad," Hurley noted.

Still, the Huskies' perimeter "D" had to improve. And he knew it.

UConn flew out to Indianapolis a couple of days later to face Butler at historic Hinkle Fieldhouse. The Huskies jumped out to a 14–2 start, but that was a distant memory by the time Boden Kapke lined up a wide-open 3-pointer with about 6½ minutes left and a chance to give the Bulldogs their first lead of the game.

It rattled in and out. Butler had other chances to take a lead down the stretch but missed free throws and open shots. UConn emerged with a 78–74 victory.

The Huskies had closed out 2024 on a six-game winning streak following Maui. At 10–3 overall and 2–0 in the Big East, they were just one game behind their overall pace from a year earlier, and actually a game ahead of where they had been in league play.

"I'm not sure how many people, at that point in Maui, were on their stupid podcasts saying we'd be 10–3," Hurley gloated. "Not all podcasts are stupid, but some of them are. Some of them say stupid shit."

Hurley was relishing the opportunity to throw some shade at all perceived doubters, of both his team and him. Still, he admitted he wasn't blameless, particularly in Maui.

"I think criticism of me, based on how hard I push from a competitive standpoint, I think some of it was warranted," he confessed to *CT Insider*. "But the people that took shots, and were waiting years for their opportunity, I guess my mistake was giving them the opening by losing three in a row."

Later that night, Hurley and Luke Murray drove roughly 30 minutes down the road to Greenfield, Indiana, to check out their prized 2025 recruit. Braylon Mullins, a gifted, 6-foot-5 guard who could shoot from all over the floor and was a deft passer and quality defender, showed all that and more in Greenfield High's blowout win over Lawrenceburg.

Mullins was the top recruit in an impressive UConn recruiting class that was ranked No. 3 in the nation at the time by 247Sports.com. He'd be joined by Eric Reibe, a 7-foot German who played at the Bullis School in Maryland and was a marksman from three-point territory;

Darius Adams, a 6-foot-5 combo guard who could also shoot (but would ultimately de-commit from UConn); and Jacob Furphy, a shooter from Tasmania who had already earned the nickname "Tazzy" from Hurley.

The Huskies had certainly honed in on shooters for this class, anticipating the losses of McNeeley and possibly Karaban to the NBA. But that was for the future. The present was looking pretty good for UConn, which had ascended to No. 9 in the AP poll entering a New Year's Day bout with DePaul in Chicago.

38

Next Man Up

Liam McNeeley had been everything the Huskies could have hoped for and more through the first two months of his freshman season. He was the team's second-leading scorer (13.6 per game) and rebounder (5.8), shot 38 percent from the three-point line, and played with confidence and maturity far beyond his age.

He was seemingly locked in a pretty good battle for Big East Freshman of the Year with Georgetown's Thomas Sorber, a 6-foot-10, 255-pound center. Sorber was at or near the top of the league in scoring, rebounding, and blocked shots. And he played for a team that was (finally) competitive, as the Hoyas jumped out to a 12–2 start under second-year coach Ed Cooley.

But all that seemed to fly out the window when McNeeley fell to the floor in obvious pain a little over 6 minutes into the second half of UConn's eventual 81–68 victory over DePaul. Trainer James Doran helped him to the bench; a few minutes later, McNeeley limped back to the locker room, mostly on his own but with some help from director of basketball administration Chris Mastrangelo.

It didn't look like an Achilles injury, but perhaps a knee? Either could sideline McNeeley for most of, if not the rest of, the season. When McNeeley returned to the bench in the final minute of the game sporting a walking boot on his right foot, it appeared to be good news. And it was. Sort of.

McNeeley was diagnosed with a high ankle sprain. It would keep him out of action for at least three or four weeks. Better than three or four months, obviously. But still not ideal.

For about the next month or so, other players were going to have to step up in McNeeley's absence.

"There's no other option, really," Karaban reasoned.

In truth, UConn had been remarkably lucky with injuries over the prior two seasons. Yes, Samson Johnson went down with a leg injury in the first game of the 2022–2023 season, missed well over a month, and was never a factor in the Huskies' title run. Still, his absence created the opportunity for Karaban to jump into the starting lineup and never relinquish it.

Andre Jackson Jr. and Adama Sanogo each missed a few games early in that season. The following year, Stephon Castle and then Donovan Clingan missed multiple games early on. Solo Ball and Johnson got valuable playing time in their stead.

But in both seasons, by the time March came around, UConn was completely healthy. Not a single scholarship player on the roster was unavailable for the NCAA tourney runs of 2023 and 2024.

McNeeley's absence could be somewhat of a mixed blessing for the Huskies. Jayden Ross, Jaylin Stewart, Aidan Mahaney, and Ahmad Nowell were among those whose roles and minutes could increase.

"It's an opportunity for the entire roster," Hurley noted.

It was Ross who got that first opportunity in a Sunday afternoon game against Providence on January 5, 2025, in Storrs. The 6-foot-7 bouncy, energetic forward barely played as a freshman and had had limited success over the first couple of months of his sophomore season. But he provided long, athletic defense out on the perimeter, something the Huskies had been searching for desperately.

Then, Providence jumped out of the gates and shot 57 percent from the floor in the first half, mostly on strong drives to the basket, to hand UConn a 39–27 halftime deficit, the Huskies' largest of the season by far.

So much for improved defense.

The Huskies battled back, led by Diarra's career-high 19 points and big baskets down the stretch from Mahaney and Tarris Reed Jr., and managed to pull out an 87–84 win. For a change, UConn went to the foul line 32 times to Providence's 23.

"We cheated death in this one," Hurley said.

Ross didn't quite look ready for prime time in his first college start, playing 12 minutes without a point or rebound. It was Mahaney, the object of intense criticism on social media and message boards through much of the season to date, who grabbed hold of the opportunity.

The 6-foot-3 junior went 4-for-5 from the floor for 15 points, his most as a Husky to date. He hit a driving bank shot with just over 9 minutes to play that brought the Huskies to within two. On Providence's next trip down the floor, Mahaney, not known for his defensive prowess, drew a charge on Ryan Mela.

Mahaney, a Lafayette, California, product, insisted that he had been oblivious to the social media criticism surrounding his play.

"I keep a tight circle, always have," he said. "My family just wants to make sure I'm doing well as a person, first and foremost."

But surely, he had heard *some* of the noise?

"The media stuff, that's never fazed me at all," he continued. "I've kind of had to deal with this now for three years. Obviously, it's a little different when you come to a bigger stage. Nonetheless, I think the things about me don't change."

UConn may have "cheated death" in its first full game without Liam McNeeley. But the Huskies were going to have to up their game three nights later against their old rival in Philadelphia.

39

Back-to-Back... Missed Free Throws?

The tables had very much turned in the UConn-Villanova rivalry over the prior couple of seasons. UConn had won the last four meetings and five of the last six, starting with that February 22, 2022, win at Hartford when Dan Hurley was ejected in the first half.

Prior to that, 'Nova had won five straight over the Huskies, most of them blowouts. One thing that remained constant through all of it—and, indeed, for the past 30 years—was that every Villanova home game (at least in front of paying fans) against the Huskies was played at the downtown Wells Fargo Center, the 20,000-seat home of the Philadelphia 76ers and Flyers. The only exception was during that COVID season of 2021, when the Huskies and Wildcats squared off at on-campus Finneran Pavilion.

But that would change this season, as Villanova hosted UConn at Finneran on January 8, 2025. The 76ers were playing at Wells Fargo that night.

While Finneran might give Villanova a better, more intimate home court advantage, UConn's biggest worry was Eric Dixon, the Wildcats' 6-foot-8, 260-pound forward. Dixon, 22, was in his sixth year at Villanova, though he had sat out his first season as a redshirt. He had contemplated going pro the prior spring but was wooed back to school with an impressive NIL package.

Dixon was also leading the nation in scoring, entering the contest at 25.9 points per game. Perhaps more impressively, the burly forward was fifth in the nation in 3-point percentage at 48.98 percent.

He was a matchup nightmare for virtually any team. Who would draw the tough assignment? Turned out, it was Jaylin Stewart's time to step up.

Stewart, who had replaced Ross in the starting lineup, gave up four years of age and college experience, two inches and 45 pounds of size, and 21 fewer points per game to Dixon. But he wasn't going to be intimidated.

"When I first found out I was matched up with him, I got locked in," Stewart recalled.

He immediately proved he belonged and, in fact, outplayed Dixon in the first half, scoring 10 points and almost single-handedly keeping the Huskies alive as they trailed 32–25 at the break. In fact, after Stewart began the game with a flourish, Villanova coach Kyle Neptune quickly took Dixon off of him on defense and had Jordan Longino guard him instead.

Meanwhile, Dixon had just 5 first-half points on 1-for-8 shooting. And that one field goal, a 3-pointer, came with Solo Ball guarding Dixon on a switch.

After a near-invisible opening half, Ball, Karaban, and Hassan Diarra came alive in the latter, ultimately rallying back from a 12-point deficit to tie the game at 59. UConn was within a point (67–66) after Ball hit Stewart on a nice look for a reverse layup with 1:20 remaining.

The score remained the same as the Huskies had several chances to take the lead over the final 24 seconds. Finally, Karaban took the ball to the hole and was fouled (on a questionable call) by Longino with 7.2 seconds left.

It's hard to believe Hurley could have picked anyone better than Karaban to go to the line for two shots and a chance to just about wrap up a victory. Karaban had been a key cog in back-to-back national championships. More important, he had never missed back-to-back free throws over his college career.

Never.

Until now.

Karaban tossed up his first foul shot. It missed. No worries, just make the second one and overtime was likely. Somehow, someway, Karaban missed the second, as well.

Villanova won 68–66. The Huskies' eight-game winning streak was over, as was their 12–0 record on the U.S. mainland.

Karaban was crestfallen, later calling it the "lowest of lows" of his college career. His teammates were there for him.

"He's still an All-American, still got back-to-back championships," Stewart reasoned. "We were like, 'Don't worry about it. Life is going to happen. Just keep going on to the next one.'"

Perhaps Hurley, as only Hurley could, offered the best perspective.

"When he feels sad tonight," the coach said after the game, "just get off the bus when we get back to campus and do what I did after Maui. Just pull your box of rings out and maybe play with your back-to-back, national championship rings and get ready for Georgetown [in three days]."

Turns out, Karaban didn't play with his title rings over the next few days. Instead, Hurley guided him through this tough time with delicate precision.

"It's like a fine line: How many meetings are you going to have?" the coach asked rhetorically. "Because if you talk too much about it, you're bringing it up and getting him to continue to think about it. Maybe it's in his mind, 'This guy keeps talking to me about it.' You share a couple of moments and you say, 'Hey Alex, your career and your life is not a fairy tale. There's going to be adversity, especially when you've done as much as you've done. You'll have a down moment or two.'"

Hurley continued: "I felt worse about him taking three shots in the first half than I did about him missing those free throws at the end of the game. You've got to end these games with no regrets. You've got to let it rip, go for it, get out there and try to dominate. You can't disappear in the first half, or play passively. You're one of the greatest players in UConn history. What's the worst that's going to happen? You go for it this year, you attack these games and, at times, you come up short? And maybe you don't become the greatest player in UConn history, maybe you're just one of the greatest? What do you have to risk?"

Karaban heeded Hurley's words. On January 11 against Georgetown in Washington, DC, he bounced back in a big way, hitting four 3-pointers for a game-high 19 points in a 68–60 UConn win that wasn't really that close.

Seated next to Hurley at the postgame podium, Karaban said, "I don't think I'd be able to have the performance I did today if it wasn't for this man right here."

40

"Best Coach in the Sport!"

UConn had a week off until returning home to face Creighton on January 18, 2025, at Gampel Pavilion. The Huskies designed their struggling defense to stop old nemesis Ryan Kalkbrenner, the 7-foot-1 center, as well as grad guard Steven Ashworth, a long-range shooter.

By and large, they accomplished those goals. But it was a different player who rose up and had a career game instead.

Jamiya Neal, who entered the game averaging 10.2 points per game, drove to the basket almost at will while also knocking down a trio of 3-pointers en route to a career-best 24 points. One defender after another (Solo Ball, Jaylin Stewart, Jayden Ross) tried to stop Neal, to little or no effect.

Creighton walked away with a 68–63 victory that snapped UConn's 28-game home winning streak, which dated back nearly two years, to a January 25, 2023, loss to Xavier.

"This team wasn't responsible for those long winning streaks," Dan Hurley was quick to point out. "The tenacious teams that were elite defensively, elite rebounding . . . those are the teams that built that long winning streak."

And clearly, Hurley believed his team lacked that tenacity, calling the Huskies "soft."

In the waning seconds of the game, with UConn trailing by three, Creighton fouled Diarra on purpose near halfcourt to prevent a potential game-tying 3-pointer. Diarra hurled up a desperation shot while being fouled, which would have sent him to the foul line for three free throws. The officials, however, ruled that the foul occurred *before* Diarra attempted his shot, meaning no free throws.

Hurley argued at the time but sang a different tune at the postgame presser.

"Today had nothing to do with [the officials]," Hurley summed up. "The officiating we've had stateside this year has been excellent."

Hurley's obvious reference was to the fact that UConn was outshot by a combined 50 free throws in three losses in Maui.

"That's why my demeanor has been what it's been in every game that hasn't been played . . . on an island," he added.

Indeed, Hurley had generally been much calmer on the sidelines since Maui, in part a result of conversations he had with people he was close to who begged him to tone it down. He took far fewer postgame barbs at officials as well.

That wouldn't last much longer.

The day before the Huskies' January 21 bout with Butler in Hartford, Hurley continued to harp on his team's lack of aggression and tenacity, even questioning himself.

"Has success softened us, has my intensity dropped, have I lost my edge?" he said he had wondered. "Have we gotten soft with our success and feel entitled to it, or we just don't have the will to earn it? We do have a lot of people that haven't won championships with us or weren't integral parts of our championships."

Hurley's frustration only grew the following night, not only with his team but . . . you guessed it . . . with the officials.

It took the Huskies overtime to vanquish a Butler team that had just come off a nine-game losing streak. Once again, opposing players drove to the basket with little resistance, particularly Jahmyl Telfort, who poured in 25 points. Solo Ball's career-high 23 points, including a go-ahead 3-pointer with about 90 seconds left in overtime, paced the victory, though it wasn't clinched until Telfort misfired on a 3-pointer at the buzzer.

But that wasn't what was most on Hurley's mind after the game.

For the fourth straight game, the Huskies were more than doubled up at the free-throw line by an opponent. Butler shot 28 free throws, UConn a mere 14.

Once again, Hurley implied that the Huskies weren't getting the respect they had earned.

"I don't think there's a program that's won as much as we've won that at times gets as bad a whistle," he noted.

That came to a head late in the first half. With UConn up by 10 points, Hurley was trying to convey a point to official Nathan Farrell when Farrell started to walk away from him. Hurley was captured on the FS1 TV broadcast shouting at Farrell: "Don't you big-time me! I'm the best coach in the [bleeping] sport!"

Just like that, Hurley found himself embroiled in another controversy, as the clip went viral and criticism rained down on him from media outlets all over.

Hurley explained after the game that he wasn't necessarily upset with the officiating crew of Farrell, Tony Chiazza, and Pat Driscoll, all of whom he termed "great refs." Rather, he was peeved by his belief that teams had been able to grab and hold UConn shooters coming off screens through much of the season.

"The TV camera likes me . . . I just wish they'd show these other coaches losing their minds at the officials in other Big East games that I'm coaching. Going into a time-out when I'm not talking to officials, I see the other coaches as demonstrative as I am."

He added, "I've created this for myself, I'm not the victim. I just wish they would not have the camera on me 90 percent of the time. Unless they feel like it's driving ratings, and more assholes on Twitter that can put clips of me from a game and they can say, 'Look at what a monster he is, he's yelling at a ref again. What a *monster*.'"

Either way, Hurley's sideline behavior once again garnered negative national attention. Later in the week, Hurley went on a podcast with 247Sports.com's Adam Finkelstein, seemingly in an effort to nip things in the bud. He noted that the only embarrassing part of his comments to Farrell that night was with his fellow coaches.

"I coach against [Xavier's] Sean Miller this weekend. When I see Sean, I'm going to be embarrassed about what I said to an official, putting myself up on that pedestal. I think that's the only place that I'm going to feel embarrassed is when I see [Michigan State] Coach [Tom] Izzo and when I see [Kansas coach] Bill Self—saying something egotistical like that relative to all the amazing coaches that are just as good or better than me as a coach."

He added, "But those are the only people that I feel any type of way toward. For me, my players love playing for me. My fans, my UConn fans, they love the way I coach."

Once again, ESPN's *GameDay* crew was critical.

"It's the constant berating of officials throughout a game that fans think are influencing calls," Jay Bilas said. "So, if it influences calls, then that's a competitive advantage, and we need to deal with it. If it doesn't influence calls, then it's really bad optics, and people have the perception that it does, and I think we need to deal with that . . . I don't think that's a very good look."

Cohost Andraya Carter added, "He can show his personality in ways that don't include belittling."

On January 25, UConn was in Cincinnati to face Miller and Xavier at Cintas Center, site of two of Hurley's more infamous technical fouls from seasons past. And the Xavier crowd was ready for him.

A large pack of students serenaded the team with "F— Dan Hurley! F— Dan Hurley!" chants. Not when the Huskies took the floor for the game that night, or when they were announced in pregame introductions, mind you.

No, those chants greeted Hurley and the Huskies *when they got off the team bus to walk into the arena*, some two hours before tip-off. And they continued, periodically, through pregame warmups, as well as when the Huskies took the floor and during pregame introductions. And throughout the game. A game that Xavier won, 76–72.

"This is a real hard place to play," Hurley said postgame. "It's also a very fun place to play. That atmosphere is like an Octagon in there. But I love it."

Perhaps, but it was clear that Hurley was hurt by the vitriol that was being hurled his way. This wasn't the kind of respect and admiration Hurley was expecting as a two-time defending national champion coach. His players felt his pain.

"For someone to chant those names at Coach, it hurt me a lot, just because he's meant everything to me these last three years," Alex Karaban told *CT Insider* a few days later. "It definitely got me mad and angry and wanting to do everything possible to get that win for him, just because I don't like people talking trash about my coach and someone I genuinely love. It definitely gets your blood boiling."

On Hurley's way back to the locker room following his postgame press conference at Xavier, I asked him if he was worried about getting similarly rude greetings from fans at upcoming games at Creighton (where the "F— Dan Hurley!" chants originated a year earlier), St. John's, and Providence.

Hurley thought about it, gave an answer, then later asked not to be quoted. He wanted to think about it some more and have me call him back the following day. That was later pushed back two days later to January 28, at the Huskies' media availability prior to a bout with DePaul in Hartford.

Prior to meeting with the rest of the media at XL Center, Hurley gave me a few minutes one-on-one.

"The only time it affects you," Hurley he said of the rude receptions, "is during an anthem when you can hear it, or when you're walking through the tunnel either way. You just don't want people going too far, leaning over railings. If they want to use expletives with my name during different points, if that's how their fan bases and programs and universities do business, then that's how they do it."

He was particularly irked at Bilas, the former Duke star, but added that none of this was really new to him.

"This has been my experience in basketball. As a high school player, college player, even throughout my coaching career, just being a Hurley. With a successful basketball family, and with the multipliers you put on top of that—the UConn brand, the historical success we've had the last two years doesn't make you beloved. It makes you a target. When you go on the road, the environments that we face are incredibly hostile. Maybe even going too far. Maybe that's why I fight so hard. Maybe that's why I coach so hard. Because I find myself in these very hostile environments—especially as the coach of a program like UConn."

The following night, as if the team was stung by the latest national criticism, UConn fell behind by 14 points in the first half to DePaul, which was 1–9 in the Big East and had lost 19 straight games to the Huskies. During one time-out, some boos rained down from the XL Center crowd. Not exactly what Hurley wanted to hear on the heels of a hostile road trip.

"I guess the fans can decide, based on everything we've given them the last two years, whether that was warranted or not," Hurley said of the booing.

The Huskies outscored the Blue Demons by 19 points in the latter half and earned the win. But nothing was coming easy lately for UConn, which had gone win-loss-win-loss-win-loss-win over its prior seven games, entering an always difficult road trip to first-place, ninth-ranked Marquette.

On National Marquette Day, of all days.

With national-champion heroes Andre Jackson Jr. and Cam Spencer among the record crowd of 18,129 at Fiserv Forum, however, the Huskies went out and had a ball. Or, more aptly, a Ball.

Solo Ball erupted for by far the best game of his college career, knocking down 7 of 9 three-pointers and finishing with a career-high 25 points, to go with a career-best 10 rebounds. Despite turning the ball over an unfathomable 25 times, the Huskies never trailed en route to a 77–69 win.

41

Meet Mr. McNeeley

UConn had a much-needed six-day respite before hosting St. John's and Rick Pitino for the first time of the season on February 7, 2025, a Friday night at Gampel. The Red Storm were 20–3 overall and 11–1 in the Big East.

The Huskies got some good news going into the game. Liam McNeeley, out since sustaining that high ankle sprain on New Year's Day, was cleared to play. He wouldn't start, coming off the bench for the first and only time of his brief UConn career, and struggled with his shot (4-for-15). But he notched a double-double with a team-high 18 points to go with 11 rebounds.

It wasn't enough, however, to prevent the Huskies' second straight loss at Gampel. And their first loss to Pitino under Hurley.

Once again, the turnovers mounted—22 in all, keyed largely by St. John's furious, full court pressure. Once again, Husky-killer Kadary Richmond (who had transferred to the Johnnies after three seasons at Seton Hall) came up with big plays down the stretch during a 12–0 run. Richmond hit RJ Luis Jr. on a pretty inbounds play for a baseline jumper with 10.1 seconds left that sealed the Johnnies' 68–62 victory.

Hurley, who just a few weeks earlier had famously proclaimed to be "the best coach in the [bleeping] sport," openly questioned himself.

"It makes you feel like you're not coaching your team well when you have 47 [combined] turnovers two games in a row," he rued. "You feel like you're a [bad] coach."

UConn's guard play was becoming a massive issue. Hassan Diarra, a gutsy veteran and the team's best defender, was battling a hip injury that might have sidelined a less tough player. Junior transfer Aidan Mahaney was struggling so much on both ends of the floor that freshman Ahmad Nowell had usurped him in the rotation off the bench. And Nowell often looked like a freshman when taking the ball up the floor against pressure "D."

All this and the Huskies, who had dropped out of the AP Top 25 rankings following the St. John's loss, now had a trip to 24th-ranked Creighton in Omaha, Nebraska, where UConn had never won since rejoining the Big East.

That's where Liam McNeeley decided to introduce himself to the world.

Back in the starting lineup, McNeeley notched one of the top performances in UConn history. The 6-foot-7 freshman shot 12-for-22 from the floor, 5-for-10 from three-point range, and 9-for-10 from the foul line for 38 points. It was the highest single-game scoring output by any UConn player since James Bouknight's 40-point effort on December 20, 2020, at Gampel Pavilion—ironically, also against Creighton.

McNeeley also grabbed 10 rebounds for the first 30–10 double-double at UConn since 2014 and the first in a Big East game since 2011.

More important, his personal, 8–0 run in the second half gave the Huskies their first lead, and his two free throws in the waning seconds clinched a 70–66 win.

"One of the best performances of the college basketball season by probably any player, at that level of a game," Hurley said.

A year earlier, McNeeley was on a Montverde Academy team whose starting lineup read like a list for the 2025 Wayman Tisdale National Freshman of the Year award. Or the 2025 NBA Draft green room.

Joining McNeeley in that starting five was Robert Wright, the starting point guard at Baylor; Asa Newell and Derik Queen, the dominant big men at Georgia and Maryland, respectively; and, of course, Cooper

Flagg, who had famously chosen Duke over UConn and was putting together a season worthy of National *Player* of the Year consideration, never mind National Freshman of the Year.

"That's the best high school team of all time right there," McNeeley said following his 38-piece.

On this night, none of those players—in fact, no player in the country—was better than Liam McNeeley.

In the moments after the victory, however, Hurley couldn't resist tempting a little more controversy. On his way to the same tunnel where he had verbally sparred with Creighton fans the prior season, he took time to rub it in to a loud, follically challenged Bluejays fan.

"Two rings, baldy!" he shouted, while pointing to his ring finger. "Bye, bye! Two rings! Two rings!"

Another viral moment in a season full of them.

42

Jersey Barrier

UConn's huge win at Creighton had helped ease the pain of the home loss to St. John's. And it appeared the Huskies' season was about to take a turn for the better.

Three of their next five games were against Big East bottom-feeders, starting with a bout against last-place Seton Hall, which had dropped nine straight games and was 1–12 in Big East play.

Surely, the Huskies would snap a bizarre, three-game losing streak at Prudential Center during which they had been haunted by Kadary Richmond's brilliance, a loss in which they trailed in just 7 seconds of action, and the prior season's Big East–opening blowout loss where Donovan Clingan got injured.

Richmond had transferred to St. John's after an NIL-money bidding war, and the Pirates couldn't adequately replace him. Seton Hall coach Shaheen Holloway, Hurley's former replacement at point guard for the Pirates, was openly frustrated by his program's lack of NIL money and, ultimately, lack of wins.

For one night, on February 15, 2025, however, the Pirates had a rare reason to celebrate, handing the Huskies a loss that may have surpassed Maui as the nadir of this most frustrating season.

UConn's troubles at point guard, its troubles guarding both the three-point line and opponents driving to the hole, its penchant for fouling, and its overall toughness issues had been well documented.

But it was another issue that had plagued the Huskies much of the season that came back to bite them against Seton Hall: inbounding the ball.

A comedy of errors ("Keystone Kops shit," as Hurley later described) trying to throw the ball inbounds at the end of regulation, then again at the end of overtime led to a shocking, 69–68 road loss to the Pirates.

Despite poor shooting, shot-clock violations, botched alley-oops, and such, UConn led by seven with 45 seconds left in regulation. But Seton Hall managed to get within three with 12 seconds left. Alex Karaban tried to inbound the ball from beneath the UConn basket, couldn't find anyone open, and managed to call a time-out just before drawing a five-second violation.

Didn't matter. After the time-out, Karaban still couldn't inbound the ball in time, this time drawing a five-second violation and turning it over to the Pirates. Dylan Addae-Wusu hit a 3-pointer with 5 seconds left, and it was on to overtime.

Up three with 48.1 seconds left in OT, Liam McNeeley took over inbounding duties and tried a long, near–full court pass to Karaban. But it was out of Karaban's reach and went out of bounds.

Isaiah Coleman hit a pair of free throws to get the Hall within a point. Karaban then inbounded to Solo Ball, but instead of holding onto the ball and getting fouled with 6 seconds left, he tried to split through a trap and turned the ball over to Garwey Dual. Scotty Middleton collected a loose ball, put up a wild shot that missed, but tipped in his own miss with 3 seconds left to put the Pirates ahead.

Hassan Diarra's desperation shot at the buzzer was off the mark, and UConn had one of its worst losses of Hurley's seven-year tenure.

"It feels like, in the end, we got what we deserved," an embarrassed Hurley said afterward. "The ramifications of this one will be felt."

Outside the losing locker room, Karaban was even more blunt.

"As a team, player-wise, we don't take every game seriously and don't treat every game life-or-death, the way the coaching staff does," the UConn captain said. "It's our fault. It's completely on the players.

We just didn't show up ready to play. We were soft the entire game. It's on us."

Karaban hit a couple of key 3-pointers in the second half to break out of what was at the time an 0-for-16 slump from distance over his prior two-plus games and 2-for-23 over his prior five-plus. He hardly absolved himself from blame.

"I was supposed to be doing that [hitting 3-pointers] for the past month," he said. "It feels good to snap out of it, but I'd rather miss all those shots and win the game."

Three nights later, the Huskies found themselves down 14 points to Villanova in Hartford with just under 12 minutes to play. They closed out the game on a 14–1 run to avoid the upset. But the Huskies' maddening, win-one, lose-one pattern continued on February 23 with an 89–75 loss to St. John's at Madison Square Garden that wasn't even that close.

The Johnnies, who entered the game dead last in the Big East and 341st out of 355 teams in the country in 3-point shooting, knocked down eight from long distance in the first half alone to build up as much as an 18-point lead and cruise to victory.

Still, UConn was able to regroup and close out its regular season on a four-game winning streak. A 93–79 win over Georgetown clinched the Huskies' second-straight undefeated season at XL Center. At Providence on March 1, Tarris Reed Jr., the Michigan transfer who spent the entire season as Samson Johnson's backup center despite putting up much better numbers, dominated with 24 points, 18 rebounds, and 6 blocks in a 75–63 win.

In an early March game with major Big East tournament seeding implications, the Huskies edged Marquette despite a delayed start due to a leaky Gampel Pavilion roof (where have we heard that before?). And on Senior Day, UConn notched that rarest of rarities, at least for the 2024–2025 season: a blowout victory. The Huskies "avenged" that crushing loss to Seton Hall a few weeks earlier with an 81–50 romp at Gampel. Samson Johnson and Hassan Diarra, who were definitely playing their final home games as Huskies, and Alex Karaban, who possibly was, carried the day.

A year after UConn had won 28 games by double digits, 11 by 30 points or more, this was just their 10th double-digit triumph of the season.

The Huskies finished their regular season 22–9 overall and 14–6 in the Big East, good for the No. 3 seed in the upcoming Big East tournament. St. John's and villainous Rick Pitino had tied UConn's record for Big East wins in a season, going 18–2 in league play a year after the Huskies had done the same. Few would question whether the 2024 Huskies were a better team than the 2025 Red Storm, but a record is a record.

And who knew? Maybe UConn was peaking at the right time, ready to make a run through the Big East tournament and put a serious charge into hopes for a three-peat that seemed to have died somewhere between Maui and Newark.

Just before the onset of postseason play, however, Hurley couldn't help but stir up a little more controversy. In an interview with the TV news show *60 Minutes*, which had been on campus with the team throughout the season, Hurley noted that "50 percent of my roster, or more, is at least considering going in the portal, if not already knows what school they're going to."

Once again, Hurley made headlines, though he was a bit miffed about this one.

"I don't get the consternation and panic and the reaction," he said at the Big East awards ceremony at Madison Square Garden. "It's been like that the last couple of years. Schools were recruiting one of our best players off the '23 championship team during the season, with promises of big NIL money. We've dealt with this after '22, losing some players. There was a giant panic in Connecticut over what the team would look like. Obviously, our response was what we've done the last two years."

For the first time in a few years, there was no consternation from Hurley over the Big East awards. In the past, whether it was Alex Karaban getting snubbed for Freshman of the Year in 2023 or Tristen Newton getting beaten out for Player of the Year in 2024, Hurley always seemed to have something to complain about. Ultimately, national championships in both years trumped any perceived individual snubs.

In 2025, Hurley agreed that St. John's Rick Pitino and RJ Luis deserved Big East Coach of the Year and Player of the Year awards, respectively. To the victors go the spoils, he's always reasoned.

Hurley certainly wasn't about to complain that Tarris Reed Jr. won the league's Sixth Man Award, becoming the second straight Husky to earn the honor after Hassan Diarra had won it in 2024. Reed, the 6-foot-10 junior who spent his first two seasons at Michigan, was a true revelation with the Huskies, averaging 9.6 points and a team-best 7.5 rebounds per game despite coming off the bench in all but one of the team's 35 games and averaging just under 20 minutes of action.

Hurley is famously loyal to his veteran players, so he inserted senior Samson Johnson, who dutifully served as Donovan Clingan's backup the year before, as the starting center from Day 1. And that never changed, even though Johnson's numbers in scoring (7.5), rebounding (3.5), and even minutes (19.4) were topped by Reed.

Reed's deft footwork, inside touch, and nose for offensive rebounding led him to dominant, double-double performances against Providence, Memphis, Georgetown, Xavier, and St. John's, among others. Off the court, he's an adept saxophone player, a gentle giant, and a deeply spiritual young man, beginning every postgame press conference with "First of all, I'd like to thank my Lord and Savior, Jesus Christ, for putting me in this position . . ."

And he's a big fan of Po Ping, the mild-mannered main character of the *Kung Fu Panda* movies.

"He can like that movie," Hurley said earlier in the season, "but I don't want that to be his alter ego. I want it to be the bear from *The Revenant*, right up until it gets shot."

Indeed, Reed's somewhat laid-back personality doesn't quite jibe with Hurley's—one of the reasons why Reed's playing time didn't always jibe with his production.

"He's just got to decide what type of bear he wants to be," Hurley said back in December 2024. "When he's a grizzly bear or a Kodiak bear or a vicious polar bear, he's incredible. He's such a nice guy and a sweetheart that sometimes doesn't play with that force and wants to be a killer."

No one questioned "Kodiak" Reed's credentials in winning the Sixth Man Award. But there was another Big East coach, one who has had plenty of complaints about UConn in the past, who was miffed by another of the league's award winners.

43

"Karma" at MSG

Liam McNeeley was named Big East Freshman of the Year, beating out Georgetown's Thomas Sorber for the honor in a vote by the league's coaches.

Throughout the first half of the regular season, McNeeley and Sorber were far and away the top two freshmen in the league. But when McNeeley suffered that high ankle sprain on New Year's Day at DePaul, ultimately sidelining him for the next eight games, it appeared Sorber would be the de facto winner of the award.

Except Sorber wound up injuring his left foot and underwent season-ending surgery in February, missing the Hoyas' final seven games. In the end, McNeeley and Sorber each won seven Freshman of the Week honors over the course of the season. McNeeley, in what turned out to be his one-and-done season in Storrs, led the Huskies in scoring at 14.5 points per game, edging out Solo Ball (14.4) and Alex Karaban (14.3). The 6-foot-7 forward was UConn's second-leading rebounder at 6.0 per game.

The 6-foot-10 Sorber also averaged 14.5 points per game, second on the Hoyas, while leading the team in rebounding (8.5).

Perhaps most important, UConn finished third in the Big East at 14–6, Georgetown seventh at 8–12. To the victors go the spoils . . .

Georgetown head coach Ed Cooley wasn't having it.

"[Sorber] had just as much production, if not more, but had a major impact, not in the Big East, nationally. *Nationally*," Cooley griped. "And he's not recognized like that? Shame on our coaches, because that kid more than earned it, more than deserved it."

Cooley, who bolted from his hometown school of Providence for Georgetown two years earlier and had been the coach most critical of UConn being invited back to the Big East, insisted that his opinion "takes nothing away from McNeeley. Nothing at all."

Hurley, who admitted he voted for Sorber (coaches can't vote for their own player), had no issue with Cooley's rant.

"I understand it. He's defending his guy," Hurley said. "I've done that. I'm still talking about Alex Karaban losing to Cam Whitmore, and I'm still bringing up Tristen Newton not getting [Player of the Year] last year."

Speaking of Whitmore, UConn's first opponent in the 2025 Big East tournament was Villanova. Despite boasting the nation's leading scorer in Eric Dixon, along with plenty of talent out of the portal via one of the league's biggest NIL budgets, the Wildcats had been a big disappointment, finishing in sixth place in the Big East at 11–9. Still, the team was talented and, of course, had beaten the Huskies at home in January and led by 14 with less than 12 minutes to go in Hartford before falling apart.

Sure enough, 'Nova started off strong behind transfer Wooga Poplar, whose season the Huskies had ended in the Final Four two years earlier when he was at Miami. Poplar was 7-for-9 from the floor for 15 first-half points that helped the Wildcats own as much as a 9-point lead and a 36–31 edge at halftime.

Villanova also was the latest foe to outshoot the Huskies from the foul line, boasting a 16–2 advantage by the break. Two of those free throws came on a technical foul called on Hurley, who vehemently disagreed with a foul called on Aidan Mahaney.

"It was calculated," Hurley later confessed. "I pick up some technical fouls that are not calculated, they're regrettable. But that was one I wanted. But I'm not sure what type of impact it had, because the free-throw discrepancy continued."

Surprisingly, it was just Hurley's second technical of the season and first since the infamous call in Maui.

It was a tie game with 8 minutes left to play when the Huskies unleashed a head-spinning run to the finish line that resembled some of the runs they had engineered a year earlier. UConn scored 7 straight points, and, after a Jordan Longino 3-pointer, went off on a 15–0 run to seal the game.

The 22–3 run wasn't quite the 30–0 run the Huskies had dropped on Illinois in the 2024 Elite Eight. But it was more than enough to clinch a 73–56 victory.

"You definitely had flashbacks of last year when we'd go on the big runs," said Alex Karaban, who finished with 18 points and 9 rebounds.

Up next was second-seeded Creighton, led by Ryan Kalkbrenner, who had joined Hall of Famer Patrick Ewing as the Big East's only four-time Defensive Player of the Year winner; ageless guard Steven Ashworth; and coach Greg McDermott, who boasted an 8–3 record against Hurley since UConn rejoined the Big East.

Creighton had beaten UConn at Gampel in January 2025, snapping the Huskies' 28-game home winning streak. The Huskies returned the favor in Omaha in February behind Liam McNeeley's 38-point masterpiece.

The rubber match, on Friday night in the Big East tourney semifinals at Madison Square Garden, was pretty much all Creighton.

The Bluejays shot a mesmerizing 18-for-24, 75 percent, from the floor in the first half. Not from the foul line, mind you. *From the floor.*

Seventy. Five. Percent.

It led to a nine-point lead at halftime that had Hurley striding purposefully, angrily, face beet-red, to the locker room, where he unloaded on the team in a diatribe that could be heard from the nearby media room, if not Brooklyn.

And his locker-room tirade didn't seem to make much of a difference as Creighton opened the latter half on a 9–3 run to balloon its lead to 17.

Ultimately, the Huskies fought back and got to within three points with 6½ minutes left. But they had dug too deep a hole, and Creighton emerged with a 71–62 victory.

A dream, UConn–St. John's Big East championship game battle the following night had been foiled.

"It feels a little dishonorable not to be able to at least fight St. John's for the tournament championship," Hurley rued afterward. "But we don't deserve to. We're not as good as we've been."

"Obviously," he later added, "our first-half defensive performance was not worthy of having a chance to play on Saturday night at MSG against a team like St. John's this year. We got exactly what we deserved."

With 1.5 seconds left in the game, Creighton's Jamiya Neal had sprinted down the floor for a slam dunk that put an emphatic ending to a game whose outcome had already been decided. Hassan Diarra immediately ran up to Neal and shoved him in the chest, and the two squared up and exchanged words before being separated.

Neal and Diarra were hit with technical fouls. UConn reserve Jayden Ross was ejected for leaving the bench. And while order was being restored and Hurley and McDermott seemed to joke about the situation, UConn assistant coach Luke Murray appeared to have words for McDermott, who responded by waving his finger at Murray.

"Jamiya shouldn't have done what he did, and he knows it," McDermott said in the postgame press conference.

"Definitely, I got caught up in the emotions of the game," Neal confessed. "I would like to apologize for that. I respect Coach Hurley and those guys over there. They have a great, great program, obviously, a two-time national champ."

Ultimately, it was no big deal. In fact, Hurley would later admit Neal's dunk, while unnecessary, was "karma" for him taunting Creighton fans ("two rings, baldy!") following that February win in Omaha.

UConn's most important item at hand was the upcoming NCAA tournament, where a chance for a three-peat, no matter how unlikely, remained.

44

A Chance at Salvation

The strangest thing had happened to UConn entering the 2025 NCAA tournament. The Huskies, the two-time defending national champion Huskies, were somehow flying below the radar.

True, Dan Hurley had been making headlines throughout the season, most recently with his comments to *60 Minutes*. There was a recent ESPN *E:60* documentary on the Huskies as well.

But as the Big Dance dawned, UConn was hardly a headline attraction. Auburn was the No. 1 overall seed, and Florida or Duke could have just as easily earned that mantle. The Huskies weren't even the top attraction at the Raleigh, North Carolina, pod site, where UConn would begin play on a late Friday night, March 21, 2025. That distinction would go to none other than old friend Cooper Flagg, whose Blue Devils were in town as the top seed from the East Region.

John Wooden's name was no longer being brought up in association with UConn. The Huskies' historic quest to become the first (and only) program to win three straight titles aside from the Wizard of Westwood back in the late 1960s/early 1970s had become an afterthought.

Quite frankly, few believed they could pull it off. Not after the defensive woes the team had all season, most recently and notably in the first half of that Big East tourney loss to Creighton.

Certainly not the NCAA Tournament Selection Committee, which seeded UConn No. 8 in the West Region, a year after tabbing it the tourney's No. 1 overall seed. That meant a first-round bout with ninth-seeded Oklahoma. A win there would almost certainly lead to a matchup with the West's top seed, Florida.

Hurley had no issues with his team's seeding.

"I think this group is relieved to be at this point of the year," he said. "Obviously, when you're an 8-seed and you're coming in with 10 losses, our confidence isn't going to be as high as last year's team that just rolled through people and believed that every game was going to play out that way."

"But," Hurley quickly added, "I think we're a dangerous team right now."

Indeed, the NCAA tournament represented a fresh start for the Huskies.

"We have not had a very good regular season, from our standards of what we're trying to accomplish," Hurley said. "But we could change the whole narrative and change the way we view this season by playing our best this month and trying to get on a run."

He continued, "We could salvage the whole year."

Oklahoma was 20–13 overall but a mere 6–12 in league play. Of course, that league was the Southeastern Conference, which sent an astounding 14 of its 16 teams to the tournament, eclipsing the record of 11 set in 2011 by the Big East. UConn finished 9–9 in league play that year, then went out and won 11 games in a row in the Big East and NCAA tournaments to capture the national title.

The first-round bout with the Sooners started a little after 9:30 p.m. A couple of hours later, the clock nearly struck midnight for the Huskies. Literally and figuratively.

Oklahoma shot just 32 percent from the floor and 3-for-19 from the three-point line. And yet, the Huskies could never quite shake the Sooners, never able to build off a 10-point lead late in the first half. A little over midway through the second half, Oklahoma took its first lead, 47–46. It would be the Sooners' only lead.

Solo Ball quickly countered with a wing jumper. UConn's lead was again just 1 point with 3:40 left when Alex Karaban, who had had a dreadful first 30 minutes of missed shots and ugly turnovers, knocked

A Chance at Salvation

down a 3-pointer. He then added a runner with 2:18 left to put the Huskies up 6 points. With 38 seconds left, Karaban blocked a Jalon Moore shot, then capped UConn's 67–59 victory with a free throw with 19.4 ticks remaining.

Just in the nick of time, Karaban, the junior captain possibly playing his final game in a UConn uniform, stepped up and saved the Huskies' season.

"You can always trust Captain America, to be honest," Ball said.

In truth, it had been a rough year for Karaban. A preseason All-American and first-team All–Big East pick, the 6-foot-8 forward wound up as UConn's third-leading scorer (14.3 points per game). He did make second team All–Big East, but he spent much of the winter in a shooting funk. After shooting 40.2 percent from the three-point line as a freshman and 37.9 percent as a sophomore, Karaban's 3-point percentage was a mere 34.7 percent. It was even worse in Big East play: 31.6 percent.

Karaban made his last-minute decision to return to UConn the prior spring with the goals of winning a third straight national title and playing himself into an NBA first-round draft pick. But by mid-March, he was viewed as a late second-round pick, at best.

Still, his late-game heroics allowed the Huskies to achieve some history. It was their 13th straight NCAA tournament game victory, starting with that opening-round win over Rick Pitino and Iona in Albany two years earlier. It was the first of those baker's dozen victories that wasn't won by double digits.

"It's hard to win a *game* in this tournament," Hurley noted. "I mean, this thing is a bear. To win 13 in a row . . ."

There was also this fact: With the victory, Samson Johnson became the all-time winningest player in UConn men's basketball history. It was the 115th win of his career, eclipsing the 114 posted previously by Rashamel Jones, Ricky Moore, and Antric Klaiber.

"It's hard to make history or do historical things at UConn," Hurley said from the postgame press conference podium. "That's crazy that a program like UConn, you've won the most games. Man . . . you're going to make me start crying."

It wouldn't be the first time that Johnson, a soft-spoken native of Togo, had brought Hurley to tears. At Senior Day a couple of weeks earlier, Hurley couldn't contain his tears while presenting Johnson his plaque alongside his parents, who had surprised him by flying in from Togo to watch him play at UConn in person for the first and only time.

"Samson is just the most awesome human being that you'll ever have in your program," Hurley continued after the Oklahoma win. "Just all about team, super talented, waiting his turn, dealt with injuries, had to earn a starting spot. He'll do absolutely anything he can to help the team win the possession."

Johnson's UConn career lived on for at least another day. To notch career win No. 116, he and the Huskies would have to dispatch an extremely deep and talented Florida team.

45

Going Out with Honor

Following his off-day press conference on Saturday, March 22, 2025, Dan Hurley mentioned out of nowhere that he had been gifted with a Carolina Hurricanes jersey by the Greater Raleigh Convention and Visitors Bureau. The Hurricanes' home arena, after all, is Lenovo Center, where the Huskies' first two tourney games were being played.

Of course, the Hurricanes are also the franchise that used to be the Hartford Whalers, the beloved former NHL team that relocated to Raleigh in 1996–1997 after 25 seasons in Connecticut.

With that in mind, Hurley opined out loud, to no one in particular, that he appreciated the gesture, but . . .

"Obviously I would never put it on. I've got to decide whether to keep it. That would be a big problem in Connecticut."

"I don't think [the bureau] understands," he continued, "that they stole our NHL team."

The operative word here was "our." Hurley, born and raised in Jersey City, high school star at St. Anthony's High in that same city, five-year point guard at Seton Hall, is Jersey to the core. Or *was* Jersey to the core.

It appeared that seven years in Connecticut had switched his "home" allegiances. He clearly loved the state, loved the fan base that had supported him throughout this most trying season, when so many other fan bases serenaded him with profane chants and were even worse on social media.

Hurley really, *really* wanted to beat Florida. For those UConn fans who loved him so much. For his players, who had gone through a rocky, up-and-down season. For his legacy. Not any more than any other opponent, any other game. But he had eyes on shocking just about everyone and somehow making that run to John Wooden territory.

And for a good portion of the game on Sunday, March 23, it looked like the Huskies just might do it.

Although UConn missed its first seven and 11 of its first 12 shots (including eight of nine misses from the three-point line) despite getting numerous open looks, the Gators couldn't adequately take advantage. When Hassan Diarra hit a long 3-pointer as the shot clock wound down, then Will Richard's corner 3 rimmed in and out at the buzzer, the game was tied at 31 at halftime.

The Huskies bounced out of the second-half gates with consecutive buckets from Samson Johnson (on a lob, then a no-look pass, both from Diarra). Johnson quickly picked up his third foul, but a Diarra and-1 put the Huskies up six.

UConn maintained the lead through much of the latter half but could never push it to more. With 2:53 left, Walter Clayton Jr. hit a 3-pointer that gave Florida its first lead of the second half, and Richard followed with a dunk off a Liam McNeeley turnover.

Solo Ball's 3-pointer tied it back up, but Florida went on an 8–0 run. Twice, the Gators missed free throws but grabbed the offensive rebounds to keep the possessions alive and, ultimately, score. Walter Clayton Jr. hit a dagger 3-pointer with about a minute to play.

At the game's final buzzer, McNeeley hit just his second 3-pointer in eight attempts on the day. It didn't matter to anybody but gamblers. Florida had escaped with a 77–75 victory.

The UConn men's basketball team's quest for a near-unprecedented third straight national title was officially over. But it went down fighting, falling to a No. 1 seed that, two weeks later, would edge Houston in the national championship game.

"We played with honor today," said Hurley, "and I love my team for that."

The Huskies shot 8-for-29 (27.6 percent) from three-point land against the Gators. McNeeley finished with a team-high 22 points for UConn but shot just 6-for-16 overall. McNeeley, Ball, and Alex Karaban, UConn's top three scorers, combined to shoot 6-for-26 from the three-point line. And one of those was that meaningless last-second 3-pointer by McNeeley.

For UConn, the shots simply didn't fall. But afterward, the tears did. Lots of them.

Hurley choked up while talking to CBS sidelines reporter Tracy Wolfson, then wept during his postgame press conference. Solo Ball openly sobbed in one corner of the locker room. In another corner, Alex Karaban was swarmed by reporters, composed—at first.

After the final game of the prior two seasons, both national title victories, Karaban was asked if his team deserved to be known as an all-time great, and he was incredulous in 2024 that the question even had to be asked.

Now, he was being asked how it felt to be ousted from the tournament's first weekend.

"We didn't think we were going to lose," he said. "It just sucks when we miss a couple of opportunities. I guarantee you, if we were playing them again, me, Liam, and Solo wouldn't shoot like that again."

Then reporters asked Karaban about his now-former teammates, Samson Johnson and Hassan Diarra, whose championship careers had officially come to a close. That's when the tears began to fall.

"Imagine a locker room without them," he posed. "Two of my favorite teammates. They gave everything they've got to UConn. It's going to be hard imagining next year not being with them, not seeing a locker room with those guys."

Did that mean Karaban intended to return for his final year of eligibility?

He said he didn't know, but added, through tears: "I don't want to take this jersey off. I really don't."

McNeeley, despite going through a shooting slump over his final couple of weeks, had played himself into a possible NBA lottery pick.

He was noncommittal about his future, other than to say his freshman season at UConn "didn't end the way I wanted it to."

A couple of weeks later, McNeeley entered the NBA Draft.

The futures were much more in question for Johnson and Diarra, neither of whom were likely going to be selected in the NBA Draft, despite Dan Hurley's "wall potential" prediction for Johnson four years earlier.

But Johnson would leave UConn as its all-time winningest player, notching a double-double in his final game. Diarra would leave as the 2024 Sixth Man Award winner who bravely battled through injuries nearly the entire ensuing season.

Both would leave as two-time national champions.

After the final buzzer of their careers had sounded, Hurley had his arms draped around the shoulders of Diarra and Johnson as the trio walked off the Lenovo Center floor. That should have been the lasting image of the Huskies' bold but unsuccessful run at history.

However, this being the wild roller coaster of a 2024–2025 season, it wasn't. Hurley found time to create one more controversy.

Groundhog Day

The UConn men's basketball team has had plenty of famous faces at their games over the years, from former players to celebrity fans. Perhaps the most notable during the Huskies' run of success has been Bill Murray.

The former Saturday Night Live cast member, comedian, and star of such films as Caddyshack, Ghostbusters, Groundhog Day, Lost in Translation, and (alongside Michael Jordan) Space Jam was a frequent attendee of UConn's Big East and NCAA tournament games between 2023 and 2025.

There was good reason, of course: Murray's son, Luke, was hired as a UConn assistant in May 2021. In fact, Bill Murray had often attended games of whatever teams had Luke on their staff: Xavier, Louisville, Rhode Island.

During his introductory Zoom call after being hired by UConn, Luke Murray admitted he preferred to be known for his own career, noting: "I'm definitely proud of my dad and his accomplishments, but at the same time, that really doesn't have a whole lot to do with me, or what I'm about on a daily basis."

Still, he promised that Pops would likely be at plenty of UConn games.

"He's a huge fan of Coach Hurley's and Coach Moore's."

Sure enough, Bill Murray was at nearly every one of UConn's NCAA tournament games during the Huskies' run at a three-peat. He was even with Luke at the 2024 NBA Draft, where Stephon Castle and Donovan Clingan were lottery picks.

Through it all, Bill Murray didn't talk much to the media, preferring to leave the spotlight to his son's team. I approached him prior to UConn's Elite Eight bout with Illinois at Boston's TD Center on March 30, 2024, asking if he had a minute just to talk about his son's accomplishments.

"No," he replied.

Alrighty then.

A year earlier, however, he had granted Fox Sports' John Fanta a brief interview following the Huskies' Elite Eight win over Gonzaga.

"I'm very proud of this boy," Murray said of Luke. "He's a wonderful kid, and he's worked very hard."

Murray took his travel miles to a different level in 2025. He was at both of UConn's Big East tournament games at Madison Square Garden on March 13 and 14. A few days later, there he was in Japan (perhaps lost in translation) to take in Major League Baseball's season-opening series between the Dodgers and his beloved Chicago Cubs.

A few days after that, Murray was in Raleigh, North Carolina, for UConn's NCAA tournament bout with Oklahoma. Unfortunately for him and the Huskies, there was no "Cinderella story" this time around.

46

One Final Act

As Hurley and his team left the floor and filed through a tunnel to their locker room following the season-ending loss to Florida, they walked by the players from Baylor, who were about to take the floor to play Duke in the nightcap of the day's doubleheader.

Hurley, out of nowhere, yelled, "I hope they don't [bleep] you like they [bleeped] us! I hope they don't do that to you, Baylor!"

It was one last parting shot by Hurley to the officials. UConn had been whistled for 21 fouls in the game, Florida 17. The Huskies shot 22 free throws, Florida 34. A significant difference but hardly as egregious as Maui or Villanova in the Big East tournament or numerous other games throughout the season. And certainly, part of the reason for the discrepancy was that UConn purposely fouled the Gators while trailing over the final minute to stop the clock and hope for missed free throws.

But Hurley felt his Huskies had gotten shafted by the refs once again. His rant was captured on cell phone video by Joey Ellis of *Charlotte Sports Live* and *Queen City News* and quickly posted on X (formerly Twitter).

"That was one last, final act there on the way out," Hurley told local reporters a few days later. "Just figured I'd close the show."

Bobby Mullen, UConn's media relations director, approached Ellis shortly afterward and threatened to ruin Ellis's life if he didn't take down the video. Ellis refused, and the video went viral. Once again, Hurley was castigated on social media and later by national media.

ESPN's Jay Williams, who had largely defended Hurley's "I'm the best [bleeping] coach in the sport" tirade a month or so earlier, called the UConn coach a "sore loser." Seth Greenberg, a frequent Hurley ally, couldn't dismiss this one.

"He can't help himself, but that's who he is," Greenberg said. "He had a poor decision, a poor choice of words. . . . He's gotta get better at that. That's unacceptable."

A story about Mullen's threats to Ellis appeared in the *New York Post*. In turn, he received hundreds of profane, derogatory messages via email and social media. Hurley later said he felt "horrible" about dragging Mullen into the controversy.

Mullen soon apologized to Ellis, but such was this crazy 2024–2025 season: UConn's media relations guy the subject of a critical story in the country's most notorious tabloid.

And yet, that wasn't Hurley's only verbal tirade in the moments following the season-ending loss. Shortly after his "one final act" in the tunnel, Hurley held an impromptu press conference with a handful of reporters outside the locker room.

When it was done, he thanked the local media, then shouted out, to no one in particular, "and not the national talking heads, the Skip Bayless wannabe's . . . and you never will be!" It was a reference to the hot-take artist who hosted ESPN's *First Take*, then Fox Sports 1's *Skip and Shannon: Undisputed* for several years.

A few days later, Hurley was still going after the national media.

"They've got to talk about something. It's probably boring to talk about, or they just don't really understand basketball to a level where they can talk intelligently about how we've been as successful as we've been. So I don't know if just the people that cover our sport don't know enough about basketball and why people win and why people lose and why people are champions and why they're not, where they're more comfortable talking about me with some of these things that, in my mind, I just don't know if they're that huge of a deal. My players love playing for me. I don't think I'm a bad guy. I'm not a victim, because I do stupid [stuff] sometimes. But it's not like I'm some phony, fake cheater."

Hurley pointed out that such outbursts and antics are nothing new for him as a coach, dating back to St. Benedict's Prep to getting booted from his own closed-door scrimmage at Rhode Island to getting ejected before a smattering of fans in Tulsa or a sellout crowd against Villanova in Hartford.

"This is what UConn knew they were getting," he reasoned. "This is how I've coached, obviously, my entire career. And I'm not bragging about that. I'm just surprised that people just discovered it, if they're college basketball experts. They could have been breaking me down the last couple of years, or even five years ago. Getting into it with fans or coaching my ass off, I've been doing this for a long time. So it's one of those things where, again, it's like there are mistakes, there are things I wish I didn't do. It's part of what you get with me. I hope to not do it again."

Ultimately, Hurley admitted that the better team had won in Raleigh, and that the referees had nothing to do with the outcome.

"We missed the shots and they made the shots, and those are three great officials on that game," Hurley said. "Although I said something in the heat of the moment in an area of the arena that, pretty much every game I've coached in college, has been media-free—past the tunnel, by the locker rooms, in the hallway where the coaches go. That's for the combatants. That's for the competitors. That's not for camera phones. Relative to that, those are three great refs and Florida earned it."

The exhausting 2024–2025 season was over. Now, some major decisions had to be made.

47

Comings and Goings

"Me season" started at UConn a little earlier than the prior couple of years on the heels of the Huskies' Round-of-32 exit. As Hurley had promised on *60 Minutes*, numerous players would be departing the program.

McNeeley declared for the NBA Draft, a surprise to no one. The rest of UConn's 2024 recruiting class was also leaving: point guard Ahmad Nowell and forward Isaiah Abraham entered the transfer portal after seeing scant playing time as freshmen. Abraham wound up staying in the Big East, heading to Georgetown to play for Ed Cooley. Nowell surfaced at Virginia Commonwealth University (VCU).

Youssouf Singare, the 6-foot-10 center who played little more than garbage time in his two seasons with the Huskies, transferred to High Point University.

Solo Ball announced he was staying. Ball had started popping up on NBA mock draft boards, so it stood to reason that he might at least test the draft waters at the NBA combine in May 2025, then decide whether to return to Storrs, as Alex Karaban had done the year before and Tristen Newton the year before that.

But if you had heard Ball's emotional sobbing in the locker room following the loss to Florida, it was evident how much he loved the program and was in no hurry to leave.

Jayden Ross, despite playing sparingly for much of the season, elected to return for his junior year. He would soon be joined by his younger brother, Jacob, a three-star recruit who committed to the Huskies in May 2025.

Perhaps most surprisingly, Jaylin Stewart also decided to come back. The 6-foot-7 forward showed promise late in his freshman season and figured to play a key role as a sophomore. But McNeeley's late commitment, followed by Karaban's decision to return, hindered Stewart's playing time.

He had his moments, never more so than at Villanova, when he kept the nation's leading scorer under wraps defensively while scoring 14 points on 6-for-9 shooting. But those moments were few and far between, and Stewart seemed a prime candidate to seek greener pastures. He'd have plenty of suitors.

Before Stewart and his family had even reached the parking lot at the Lenovo Center following the loss to Florida, programs were reaching out to him and his family. At least one of them was much closer to his Seattle home.

But Stewart loved his coaching staff, his teammates, the program, and the school. And he was fiercely loyal to all, perhaps more than they even knew. Knowing that a big junior season could offset a somewhat disappointing sophomore campaign, and hoping to be utilized the best way possible, he wound up being the first player to announce his return.

With Stephon Castle out in San Antonio, where he won 2025 NBA Rookie of the Year honors, UConn's vaunted 2023 "Fab Five" recruiting class was now down to three.

Less surprising, Aidan Mahaney elected to reenter the transfer portal a year after leaving Saint Mary's for Storrs. It just never worked out for Mahaney at UConn, and he wound up back out on the West Coast at UC–Santa Barbara.

But after some deliberation, Tarris Reed Jr., the Kodiak bear himself, elected to stay in Storrs. After spending his first season at UConn backing up Samson Johnson, despite putting up superior numbers, Reed figured to slot right into the Huskies' starting center spot and have a chance to have a big senior season.

Then, there was the biggest question of all: Alex Karaban. For the second straight year, Karaban was torn between returning to UConn to chase another national title or chase his dream of playing in the NBA. After going through the draft process in the spring of 2024, Karaban received no assurances that he'd be a first-round pick. More likely a second-rounder, if at all. He returned to Storrs.

A year later, after a somewhat disappointing junior season, his draft stock hadn't changed much at all. This time, he wasn't going to go to the NBA combine or test the draft waters. And he wasn't going to wait until the deadline around Memorial Day, either.

Karaban was either going to commit to another year in Storrs or go pro. And on April 29, 2025, nearly a month earlier than when he had made his decision in 2024, Karaban announced his decision.

"After deliberating the last few weeks with my coaches and family about my future," he wrote in a social media post, "I've realized that my heart remains in Storrs, and I have unfinished business to chase another national championship with my brothers. Let's run it back one last time!"

Karaban would, indeed, not "take this jersey off" for another year.

48

From Hunted Back to Hunter

Alex Karaban's decision to return, along with the returns of Solo Ball, Tarris Reed Jr., Jaylin Stewart, and Jayden Ross, quickly vaulted the Huskies into the early conversation for 2025–2026 national championship favorites.

And there was plenty more talent on the way. With Hassan Diarra graduating and Ahmad Nowell and Aidan Mahaney transferring, the Huskies needed a point guard. Preferably a bigger one. They quickly found one through the portal.

When associate head coach Kimani Young first met Silas Demary Jr., a 6-foot-5 point guard from Georgia, during Demary's official visit to Storrs on April 1, he exclaimed: "Man, there goes my PG [point guard]!"

It didn't take long for Demary, who averaged 13.5 points per game as a sophomore while leading Georgia to an NCAA tourney berth, to become Young's "PG" and commit to UConn. Certainly, Demary became an instant hit with UConn fans right off the bat after his introductory Zoom call with media.

"I want to be the next great point guard," he said. "Obviously, guys that won back-to-back, great guards like Tristen Newton, Stephon Castle, you look back even farther, Shabazz Napier, Kemba Walker. I want to be one of those names. I want to be part of a program that's been about winning."

With the 6-foot-2 Diarra, 6-foot-3 Mahaney, and 6-foot Nowell, the Huskies had been small at point guard in 2024–2025. At 6-foot-5, with a good long distance stroke (37.4 percent from the three-point line), strong defensive play, and an ability to get to the foul line and hit his free throws (127-for-158, 80.4 percent), Demary checked many of the same boxes that Mr. Triple Double himself, Tristen Newton, had checked.

"I would definitely say that's a fair comparison," Demary said of Newton. "When he was there, he had an incredible jump, coming from ECU to UConn, winning that ring. . . . Looking at his growth from where he came from . . . it was a great thing for me to see, because we have a lot of the same similarities and traits."

And there was this: Demary chose the Huskies over St. John's, the program he had visited the day before his visit to Storrs. UConn finally had another victory over the Johnnies after going 0–2 against them during the season.

A little over a week later, the Huskies got a commitment from a veteran player out of the portal who would likely serve primarily as Demary's backup. Malachi Smith, a 6-foot point guard, had spent the prior four years at Dayton, earning a medical redshirt after suffering a season-ending knee injury just 7 minutes into the 2023–2024 season.

As a senior in 2024–2025, Smith averaged 10.4 points and 5.3 assists per game as Dayton's starting point guard. Yes, that means he was part of the Flyers team that trounced UConn 85–67 in the final of the Huskies' three straight losses at the Maui Invitational. Smith scored 9 points in that one.

He beat 'em. Now, he'd join 'em.

The signings of Demary and Smith, however, would lead to somewhat of a surprise departure. Darius Adams, one of UConn's three incoming McDonald's All-Americans, saw the writing on the wall that playing time would likely be sparse for him as a freshman. In a mutual decision, Adams backed out of his commitment to the Huskies shortly after the McDonald's All-American game, and wound up at Maryland.

But the Huskies' incoming recruiting class was still very strong. Braylon Mullins, the 6-foot-5 shooting guard out of Greenfield, Indiana, was a national top-15 recruit who figured to vie for a starting role right off the bat at UConn.

On April 29, 2025, after averaging 32.9 points per game and shooting 47.6 percent from three-point territory for the season at Greenfield High, Mullins was named Indiana's Mr. Basketball, a prestigious honor never before bestowed on a UConn recruit.

Eric Reibe, the 7-footer from Germany via the Bullis School in Maryland, was sidelined by an ankle injury for much of the 2024–2025 season. But he returned in time to lead the Bullis School to the Maryland state title and earn Player of the Game honors in the championship game.

Reibe seemed a good bet to slot into the backup center's role behind Tarris Reed Jr. as a freshman in 2025–2026, similar to how Donovan Clingan backed up Adama Sanogo as a freshman in the 2022–2023 title season. But that's where the Clingan comparisons would likely end: Reibe is a much more versatile offensive player who can put the ball on the floor like a guard and shoot well from three-point range. The idea that he'd be the type of defensive game-changer as Clingan was as a frosh, however, seemed unlikely.

Reibe (pronounced "Rye-buh") quickly showed UConn fans why he considered himself, according to his high school coach, a "Dan Hurley guy." Reibe closed out his October 2024 press conference announcing his commitment to UConn by saying, "I'm happy to be a f—ing Husky!"

"I loved it," Hurley would, predictably, tell *CT Insider* later in the season.

Jacob Furphy, the 6-foot-6 swingman from Tasmania, figured to be a bit of a wild card for 2025–2026. But he also appeared to be a "Dan Hurley guy," even though Hurley had never met him or seen him play live throughout his recruitment. The phone conversations between the two, however, veered in all sorts of directions.

"Do you see any kangaroos?" Hurley once asked Furphy, who also had to convince his soon-to-be coach that a Tasmanian devil was actually a real animal.

With a solid, 10-man rotation seemingly set in stone for 2025–2026, Hurley and his staff shifted their focus to filling the team's final few scholarships. Tom Moore, the longtime assistant who was moving over to a general manager's role, told reporters on a May 4, 2025, Zoom call that the remainder of UConn's 2025 recruiting class would look "drastically different" than years past.

The departures of Ahmad Nowell and Isaiah Abraham after relatively scant playing time, along with the de-commitment of Darius Adams, highlighted the fact that there was a delicate balance in bringing in too many high-level recruits each year.

Sure, there would always be playing time for the likes of Stephon Castle and Liam McNeeley, and probably Braylon Mullins and Eric Reibe. But after that, it was tough to promise playing time to the next level of recruits, guys ranked in the top-20-to-50 range. Certainly not with the ability for teams to bring in a few high-level veteran transfers each year.

"It does feel like we may get away from bringing in huge freshmen classes," Moore said. "It'll probably be a few more elite high school prospects that have the potential to be one-and-dones, and maybe less guys that will fill out a class. So we can reevaluate at the end of the year, and maybe take one extra transfer."

And so, UConn set its sights on players—either out of high school, the portal, or the international market—who were perhaps underrecruited or underrated. Essentially, guys who would function as depth pieces and practice players, at least at first. The staff would never limit a recruit's potential to work hard and play his way into the rotation down the road.

But Dan Hurley was ecstatic with his projected 10-man rotation for the 2025–2026 season.

Alex Karaban, Solo Ball, Tarris Reed Jr., and Silas Demary Jr. were all potential All–Big East players and 2026 NBA Draft picks. Jaylin Stewart and Jayden Ross had the possibility to make big leaps as juniors. Malachi Smith seemed to have the potential to be UConn's third straight Big East Sixth Man Award winner. Braylon Mullins, Eric Reibe, and perhaps Jacob Furphy could provide help right away.

That's a roster with a lot of talent and experience, youth and potential, positional depth and versatility. And this time, the burden of winning a third straight national title wouldn't be hanging over their heads.

"It'll be nice," Hurley noted, "to go back to hunting, and not being hunted."

Epilogue

On April 5, 2025, at the Final Four in San Antonio, Houston rallied back from a 14-point deficit with 8 minutes left to beat Duke and Cooper Flagg in the Final Four. As if that didn't provide UConn fans and, perhaps, Hurley with some satisfaction, two nights later Florida edged Houston for the national championship. The Huskies could now say their season had been ended by the eventual national champs (not to mention the only program prior to theirs to win consecutive national titles).

In the day between, the UConn women's basketball team won its remarkable 12th national title, though its first since 2016, in dominating style.

Still, for the first time in nearly a year (364 days, to be exact), the UConn men's basketball team could no longer say it was the two-time defending national champion. Two-time champion, of course. Heck, six-time champion. But two-time *defending* champion? That ended around 11 p.m. on Monday, April 7.

For the first time in 735 days, the Huskies weren't even a one-time defending champion.

UConn's reign was over. But what a wild, historic ride it had been.

Dominance in Portland, Oregon, mayhem in Maui. Vomit-stained hotel rooms and stolen laptops in Las Vegas. Bad calamari in Houston. The Man in the Red Blazer at Madison Square Garden, Larry David in Boston. Bill Murray everywhere. A strange amalgam of Billy Joel, LeBron James, Magic Johnson, and Jimmy Kimmel during Dan Hurley's brief flirtation with the Lakers.

So many viral moments, good and bad: "I'm the best coach in the [bleeping] sport!" "Two rings, baldy!" "Foot stays on gas!" "I hope they don't [bleep] you like they [bleeped] us, Baylor!" "We've got our own!"

Hurley's lucky M&M's, burning sage, and of course . . . underwear.

Most of all, there was dominance. Thirteen straight NCAA tournament game victories, 12 of them by double digits. A 37–3 record and record 18 Big East wins in 2023–2024; a program-record 68 wins over the two national championship seasons. The first back-to-back men's basketball national champs in 17 years.

Ultimately, UConn's quest for a third straight national title fell a few games short. But the Huskies made plenty of history along the way.

What a ride it was.

Index

AAC (American Athletic Conference), 4, 20–21, 24, 26–27
Abraham, Isaiah, 158, 235
Adams, Bendan, 14, 17
Adams, Darius, 192, 240
Adams, Jalen, 14–16
Akok, Akok, 63–65
Alabama Crimson Tide, 70, 144–45
Allen, Teddy, 57–58, 59
Alleyne, Nahiem, 60, 97, 109–10, 120
Altieri, Tricia, 101
American Athletic Conference (AAC), 4, 20–21, 24, 26–27
Arkansas Pine-Bluff, 118
Arkansas Razorbacks, 85, 87–89
Ashton-Langford, Makai, 13
Auriemma, Geno, 69, 167–68, 169, 245

Ball, Solo: 2023–2024 regular season, 109, 114, 117, 194; 2024–2025 regular season, 158, 176, 190, 198, 201, 202, 206, 212, 217; 2025 NCAA tournament, 226, 227; recruiting, 102–4; returning to UConn, 235

Battle 4 Atlantis, 49–50, 181
Baylor Bears, 183–84, 231
Bazant, Jordan, 11
Benedict, David, 11, 87, 181–82
Big East Conference: 2023 tournament, 80–82; 2024 tournament, 133–34; 2025 tournament, 214–16, 217, 218–20; awards, 80, 214–15; changes in, 4–5, 23–27; Hurley's goals in, 55–56, 80, 123–24, 129; Media Day, 68; preseason polls, 110–11. *See also specific Big East teams*
Big 12 Conference, 123
Bilas, Jay, 177, 204
Blaney, George, 10
Boeheim, Jim, 15
Borges, David, x–xi
Bouknight, James: 2019–2020 regular season, 39, 60; 2020–2021 regular season, 35–36, 39, 208; 2021 NCAA tournament, 42; NBA and, xi, 35, 42, 105; recruiting, 26, 48–49, 54, 92; suspension, 1, 3–4
Bristol Central High School, 44–45
Brown, Javonte, 88–89
Brown, Taliek, 125–26

247

"Bubbleville" tournament, 34–35
Buss, Jeanie, 162
Butler Bulldogs: 2022–2023 season, 70, 77; 2023–2024 season, 121; 2024–2025 season, 183, 191, 202–3

Calcaterra, Joey (Joey California), 60–61, 70, 81, 99–100, 110
Calhoun, Jim, 13, 58–59, 68–69, 96, 168
Carlton, Josh, 22, 64
Carnesecca, Lou, 30–31
Carolina Hurricanes, 225
Carter, Andraya, 204
Castle, Quannette, 102
Castle, Stephon: 2023–2024 regular season, 109, 114, 115, 117, 120, 126, 194; 2024 Big East tournament, 131, 137; 2024 NCAA tournament, 141, 145, 150; awards, 131; injuries, 194; NBA and, 156, 157, 159, 236; recruiting, 102–3, 169
Central Connecticut Blue Devils, 33–34
Clemson Tigers, 95
Clingan, Donovan: 2021–2022 regular season, 60; 2022–2023 regular season, 70, 76, 183; 2023–2024 regular season, 109, 116, 118, 119, 122, 126, 183; 2024 Big East tournament, 134, 137; 2023 NCAA tournament, 97–98;

2024 NCAA tournament, 141, 145, 147–50; connection to Cooper Flagg, 106; injuries, 194; NBA and, 156, 157, 159; Phil Knight Invitational, 70; recruiting, 44–46
Clingan, Stacey Porrini, 44–45
Cole, R. J., 55, 57
Colorado Buffalos, 178
Cooley, Ed, 25, 217–18
COVID-19 pandemic: 2020–2021 season, 33–38; Borges' coverage during, x–xi; cancellations and postponements, 4, 21–22, 51; masking and, 34; recruiting during, 47–48
Creighton Bluejays: 2020–2021 season, 35; 2021–2022 season, 55, 56; 2022–2023 season, 74–75, 79–80, 82; 2023–2024 season, 122, 127–28; 2024–2025 season, 164, 201–2, 208–9, 219–20; rankings, 110–11
Cuff, Dalen, 177

Daly, Ryan, 3
David, Larry, 142
Dawkins, Johnny, 16
Dayton games, 178–79, 183
Demary, Silas, 239–40
DePaul Blue Demons: 2021–2022 season, 55; 2022–2023 season, 78, 80; 2024–2025 season, 183, 206; in "Catholic Seven," 4–5

Diarra, Hassan: 2022–2023 regular season, 77, 88, 97, 99; 2023–2024 regular season, 99, 109, 110, 118, 131; 2024–2025 regular season, 158, 182–83, 195, 198, 202, 212, 213; 2025 Big East tournament, 220; 2025 NCAA tournament, 226; injuries, 208, 228; Karaban on, 227; NBA and, 228; recognition of, 131, 182; recruiting, 60; technical fouls, 220
Diarra, Mamadou, 14, 60
Dixon, Eric, 197–98
Doran, James, 176
Duke Blue Devils, 95, 106–8, 111–12, 231
Durham, Juwan, 13
Dutcher, Brian, 139

East Carolina University, 39
East Texas A&M program, 173
Edey, Zach, 147–50
Ellis, Joey, 231–32
Enoch, Steve, 13
Ewing, Patrick, 25

"Fab Five," 102–4. *See also* Ball, Solo; Castle, Stephon; Ross, Jayden; Singare, Youssouf; Stewart, Jaylin
Few, Mark, 139, 189
Finkelstein, Adam, 203–4
Flagg, Cooper, 106–8

Florida Gators, 4, 70, 111–12, 226–27
Floyd, Corey, Jr., 81, 89
foul-shooting contests, 175
Furphy, Jacob, 192

Gaffney, Jalen, 92
Gampel Pavilion, 1–2, 53, 95
George Mason Patriots, 91
Georgetown Hoyas: 2021–2022 season, 55; 2022–2023 season, 70, 79; 2023–2024 season, 121, 123, 127; 2024–2025 season, 193, 200, 213, 217–18; Akok playing for, 64; in "Catholic Seven," 4–5. *See also* Cooley, Ed; Ewing, Patrick
Gilbert, Alterique, 14
Gonzaga Zags, 89–90, 118, 189–90
Greenberg, Seth, 177–78

Haith, Frank, 16
Hartford Whalers, 225
Hawkins, Jordan: 2021–2022 regular season, 50, 60; 2022–2023 regular season, 70, 76, 77, 80, 81, 82; 2023 NCAA tournament, 84–85, 90, 92–93, 96; NBA and, 97, 105, 109; recruiting, 47
Houston, 17, 21
Hurley, Andrea, 11, 162, 163, 185–87
Hurley, Andrew, 153–54

Hurley, Bob, Sr., ix, 8, 167
Hurley, Bobby, ix, 95, 144
Hurley, Dan: awards, 131, 147; background, ix–x, 2, 9–11, 23–27, 29, 95; blueprint for success, 8–10; on championship, 150–51; dominance of, 96–97, 112, 150–51, 245–46; hostile crowds and, 204–6, 209; love of Connecticut, 225–27; media and, ix, x–xi, 37–38; mess inherited by, 7–8; officials and, 203–4, 231–33; other teams wooing, 161–64; Pitino and, 125–26; recruitment strategies after NCAA loss, 59; relationships with players. *See specific players*; superstitions of, 29–31, 133; technical fouls and ejections, 15–16, 54, 73, 132, 171–73, 176, 218–19, 233. *See also* UConn 2018–2019 season; UConn 2019–2020 season; UConn 2020–2021 season; UConn 2021–2022 season; UConn 2022–2023 season; UConn 2023–2024 season; UConn 2024–2025 season; UConn 2025 recruits
Husky Ticket Project, 187

Illinois Illini, 140–42
Iona, 83–85, 133
Iowa, 15

Jackson, Andre, Jr.: 2021–2022 regular season, 55, 57, 59–60; 2022–2023 regular season, 70, 76, 194; 2023 NCAA tournament, 84; injuries, 194; NBA draft and, 97, 105, 109; recruiting, 26, 47, 101
Jackson, Vance, 13
James, LaBron, 162–63
Jimmy V Classic, 117–18
Johnson, Andre, Jr., 137, 154, 194
Johnson, Magic, 162
Johnson, Samson: 2023–2024 regular season, 109, 114, 120, 126, 183, 194; 2024–2025 regular season, 158, 177, 183, 189–90, 213; 2024 NCAA tournament, 149; 2025 NCAA tournament, 223–24, 226; Hurley's loyalty to, 215; Karaban on, 227; NBA draft and, 228; potential of, 47; recruiting, 54

Kansas Jayhawks, 68–69, 114–16
Karaban, Alex: 2021–2022 regular season, 60; 2022–2023 regular season, 70, 79, 80; 2023–2024 regular season, 109, 114, 118, 121, 126, 128; 2024–2025 regular season, 179, 182, 184, 190, 194, 198–200, 212–13, 217; 2024 Big East tournament, 134, 137; 2025 Big East tournament, 219; 2023 NCAA tournament, 93, 97; 2024 NCAA

tournament, 141, 145, 149–51; 2025 NCAA tournament, 222–24, 227; on Hurley, 200, 205; individual honors eluding, 80, 156–57, 170; injuries, 179, 184; NBA Draft and, 156–58; returning to UConn, 237; on teammates, 227
Kentucky Wildcats, 161–62
Knight, Bob, 168

Laettner, Christian, 95
Larranaga, Jim, 91–92
Legends Classic, 34–35
Le Moyne program, 173
Los Angeles Lakers, 161–63

Mahaney, Aidan: 2024–2025 regular season, 182–83, 195, 208; 2025 Big East tournament, 218; leaving UConn, 236; recognition of, 170
Marquette Golden Eagles: 2021–2022 season, 50, 51; 2022–2023 season, 75, 79, 80, 81–82; 2023–2024 season, 122, 128, 133–34; 2024–2025 season, 164, 206, 213; in "Catholic Seven," 4–5; ranking in preseason, 110–11
Martin, Tyrese: 2021–2022 regular season, 54, 58; fouls, 171; NBA draft and, 105
Maryland-Eastern Shore, 181

Maryland Terrapins, 41–42
Maui Invitational, 174, 175–79, 191
McDermott, Greg, 220
McNeeley, Liam: 2024–2025 regular season, 183, 189, 207, 208–9, 212, 219; 2025 NCAA tournament, 226–27; fouls, 176–77; injuries, 193–94, 217; NBA draft and, 227–28, 235; recognition of, 170, 217–18; recruiting, 158–59, 169
the media, 231–33
Memphis game, 176–77
Miami Hurricanes, 91–93
Michigan State Spartans, 50
The Miracle of St. Anthony (Wojnarowski), 43
Moore, Tom, 44, 48, 76–77, 84, 155, 242
motivation with 45:07, 49
Mullen, Bobby, 231–32
Mullins, Braylon, 240–41
Murray, Bill, 48, 100, 229–30
Murray, Luke: 2022–2023 regular season, 76–77; 2024–2025 regular season, 155; as Bill Murray's son, 229; on Edey, 147–50; UConn recruitment and, 48, 191
Musselman, Eric, 88

name, image, and likeness (NIL) money, 111, 169, 181–82, 197, 211

National Invitational Tournament, 58
NBA Draft, 105
NCAA: All-Tournament Team, 96, 150, 156–57; cancellation of games, 4; programs with back-to-back wins, 111; rankings, 113–14, 146; Selection Committee, 135–36; Selection Sunday, 56, 67–68, 82, 83; transfer portal, 88–89, 99, 168–69; UConn dominance in, 96–97, 245–46
NCAA tournament in 2006, 91
NCAA tournament in 2023: Championship, 93–94, 96–98; Elite Eight, 85, 89–90; Final Four, 91–94; First Round, 83–85; Second Round, 85; Sweet Sixteen, 85, 87–89
NCAA tournament in 2024: Championship game, 146, 147–50; Elite Eight, 140–42, 219; Final Four, 143–45; First Round, 136; flight issues, 143–44; Second Round, 136–37; Sweet Sixteen, 139–42
NCAA tournament in 2025, 221–28, 245–46
NET (NCAA Evaluation Tool) rankings, 113–14
Never Forget Tribute Classic, 50
New Mexico State Aggies, 56, 57–59

Newton, Tristen: 2021–2022 regular season, 60; 2022–2023 regular season, 69–70, 73, 76–77, 79; 2023–2024 regular season, 109, 114, 115–16, 118, 120, 127, 128; 2024 Big East tournament, 131, 132, 134, 137; 2023 NCAA tournament, 85, 96; 2024 NCAA tournament, 141–42, 150, 169; Demary comparison, 240; exhausting eligibility, 156; NBA Draft and, 157, 159; as transfer, 169
NIL (name, image, and likeness) money, 111, 169, 181–82, 197, 211
North Carolina (NC) State, 35, 117–18
Northern Arizona game, 113
Northwestern University, 136–37
Nowell, Ahmad, 158, 208, 235

Oats, Nate, 144–45
O'Grady, Dan, 132–33
Oklahoma Sooners, 222–24
Oklahoma State Cowboys, 71
Ollie, Kevin, 2, 7, 13–14, 19, 42, 43
Oregon Ducks, 69–70

Pelinka, Rob, 162
Phil Knight Invitational, 68–71, 80

INDEX

Pitino, Rick, 83–85, 124, 125–26, 136, 139, 215. *See also* St. John's Red Storm
Pittsburgh offer, 11
Polley, Tyler, 22, 36, 50, 55
Providence Friars: 2021–2022 season, 50, 51; 2022–2023 season, 74, 80–81; 2023–2024 season, 124, 129; 2024–2025 season, 183, 194–95, 213; in "Catholic Seven," 4–5; Hurley (Andrea) and, 186. *See also* Cooley, Ed
Purdue Boilermakers, 146, 147–50

rankings: 2023–2024 season, 121–22, 128; 2024–2025 season, 170, 182, 192; Associated Press, 170, 174; Big East coaches, 170; preseason, 110–11; UConn 2025 recruits, 191–92
recruitment: art of, 101–4; competition in, 25–26; Flagg deciding between Duke and UConn, 106–8; Hurley avoiding violations in, 43–44; Murray and, 48, 191; transfer portals, 88–89, 99, 168–69. *See also specific UConn players*
Reed, Tarris, Jr.: 2024–2025 regular season, 183–84, 190, 195, 213; 2025 Big East, 215; personality, 215–16; recruiting, 155; returning to UConn, 236

Reibe, Eric, 155, 191, 241
Ross, Jayden: 2023–2024 regular season, 109; 2024–2025 regular season, 158, 194–95, 201; 2025 Big East tournament, 220; recruiting, 102–4; returning to UConn, 236; technical fouls, 220
Rothstein, Jon, 10
Rutgers Scarlet Knights, 136

Saatva Empire Classic, 114
Saint Mary's Gaels, 85
Sampson, Kelvin, 21
San Diego State Aztecs, 93–94, 96, 139–40
Sanogo, Adama: 2020–2021 regular season, 36–38; 2021–2022 regular season, 47, 50, 59–60; 2022–2023 regular season, 70, 74–75, 76, 80, 81–82, 183, 194; 2023 NCAA tournament, 84–85, 93, 96; fouls, 171; injuries, 194; NBA and, 97, 105, 109; as preseason Player of the Year, 68; recruiting, 26, 54
Seattle Tip-Off, 118
Selection Sunday, 56, 67–68, 82, 83
Self, Bill, 114–16
Seton Hall Pirates: 2021–2022 season, 55; 2022–2023 season, 76–77, 80; 2023–2024 season,

253

122, 129; 2024–2025 season, 211–14; in "Catholic Seven," 4–5; Hurley playing at, 2, 10, 23, 24; Willard coaching, 25
Shows, Doug, 171
Singare, Youssouf, 103–4, 235
Smart, Shaka, 79
Smith, Malachi, 240
Sorber, Thomas, 217–18
South Florida, 15–16, 17
Spencer, Cam: 2023–2024 regular season, 110, 115–16, 117–18, 128–29; 2024 Big East, 132; 2024 NCAA tournament, 150, 169; exhausting eligibility, 156; NBA and, 100, 129, 157, 159; playing at Rutgers, 136
St. Benedict's Prep, 10, 112
Stetson, 136
Stewart, Jaylin: 2023–2024 regular season, 109; 2024–2025 regular season, 158, 182, 189–90, 198, 201, 236; 2024 Big East tournament, 134; recruiting, 103–4; returning to UConn, 236
St. John's Red Storm: 2020–2021 season, 36; 2022–2023 season, 75–76, 80; 2023–2024 season, 119–20, 122, 124; 2024–2025 season, 164, 207–8, 213; Alleyne transferring to, 109; in Big East tournaments, 131–33; in "Catholic Seven," 4–5. *See also* Pitino, Rick

St. Joseph's Hawks, 2, 3
superstitions, 29–31, 133
Syracuse Orange, 15

technical fouls and ejections, 54, 73
Texas Longhorns, 183, 184
Timberlake, Nick, 110, 116
transfer portals, 88–89, 99, 168–69
Tulane game, 21
Tulsa game, 16–17

UConn 2018–2019 season, 2–3, 13–17
UConn 2019–2020 season, 3–5, 19–22, 23, 26–27
UConn 2020–2021 season, 39–42. *See also* COVID-19 pandemic; *specific opponents*
UConn 2021–2022 season, 47–51. *See also specific opponents*
UConn 2022–2023 season: challenges, 67; Hurley's superstitions, 30; injuries, 194; January meltdown, 73–78; Phil Knight Invitational, 68–71; rankings, 70; Selection Sunday, 67–68. *See also specific opponents*
UConn 2023–2024 season: dominance, 150–51; first Big East games, 118–20; Hurley's superstitions, 30; non-conference play, 113–18;

Index

recruiting for, 101–4. *See also specific opponents*
UConn 2024–2025 season: early games, 182–84; Hurley's superstitions, 30–31; injuries, 193–94; Maui Invitational, 174, 175–79; scheduling, 181–82; transfers after, 235, 236. *See also specific opponents*
UConn 2025 recruits, 191–92, 239–43
UConn football, 25
UConn women's basketball, 69, 167–68, 169, 245
Underwood, Brad, 141
University of Central Florida Knights, 16
University of Rhode Island Rams, 9–11, 29, 186–87
University of Southern California Trojans, 35

Vanderbilt game, 35
Villanova Wildcats: 2018–2020 games with UConn, 19–20; 2021–2022 season, 51, 53–56; 2022–2023 season, 70, 80; 2023–2024 season, 122; 2024–2025 season, 164, 183, 197–99, 213; 2025 Big East tournament, 218–19; in "Catholic Seven," 4–5; historical view of, 20–21, 197; rankings in preseason, 111; Wright on Huskies in Big East, 26
Virginia Commonwealth University, 50
Vital, Christian, 4, 14, 17, 21–22

Wagner Seahawks, 10, 173–74
Werth Family Champions Center, 7, 13, 47
Whaley, Isaiah, 22, 42, 57
Willard, Kevin, 25, 139
Williams, Kwintin, 7, 14
Wilson, Sid, 17
Wojnarowski, Adrian, 43, 162
Wolfson, Tracy, 227
Wong, Isaiah, 92, 93
Wooden, John, 164, 165, 167–70
Wright, Jay, 26

Xavier Musketeers: 2022–2023 season, 73–74, 77; 2023–2024 season, 123, 124, 171–72; 2024–2025 season, 183, 190–91, 204–5; Big East tournaments, 131
XL Center, 53

Young, Kimani, 54–55, 155, 172

Zoom calls, 34, 37–39

www.ingramcontent.com/pod-product-compliance
Lightning Source LLC
Chambersburg PA
CBHW060509080526
44584CB00015B/1611